How to Open and Operate a Restaurant

A Step-by-Step Guide to Financial Success

How to Open and Operate a Restaurant

A Step-by-Step Guide to Financial Success

Ray Petteruto

VAN NOSTRAND REINHOLD COMPANY
NEW YORK   CINCINNATI   ATLANTA   DALLAS   SAN FRANCISCO
LONDON   TORONTO   MELBOURNE

Van Nostrand Reinhold Company Regional Offices:
New York Cincinnati Atlanta Dallas San Francisco

Van Nostrand Reinhold Company International Offices:
London Toronto Melbourne

Library of Congress Catalog Card Number: 79-11215
ISBN: 0-442-24870-9

Manufactured in the United States of America

Published by Van Nostrand Reinhold Company
135 West 50th Street, New York, N.Y. 10020

Published simultaneously in Canada by Van Nostrand Reinhold Ltd.

15 14 13 12 11 10 9 8 7 6 5 4 3 2 1

658.91
Petteruto

Library of Congress Cataloging in Publication Data

Petteruto, Ray.
    How to open and operate a restaurant.

    Includes index.
    1. Restaurant management.   I. Title.
TX911.3.M27P47   658'.91'64795   79-11215
ISBN 0-442-24870-9

I Dedicate This Book
To June, My Wife
And Susan, My Daughter

Preface

Have you ever had the American feeling of wanting to own and operate your own restaurant? Have you ever wanted to be the manager? Do you want to improve your present food service position? Are you a student, teacher, lawyer, housewife, astronaut, Indian chief, doctor, or anyone else who wants to go into the food service industry at any level? If you are a person with a lot of energy, not afraid of hard work, can handle financial detail, and enjoy working with people, chances are good that you might find a profitable and satisfying career in the food service industry. It is the third largest industry in the U.S. and is still growing. Sales in 1978 were estimated at close to $100 billion. Many good employment and business opportunities exist for the well-trained person, either as a chef, cook, pastry chef, manager, entrepreneur or in other capacities. The problem has always been to find qualified people who cannot only adapt to circumstances and events, but also have the ability to interact with others.

This book was not intended to be full of theory, charts, questions, or a great deal of statistical data. Its main objective is to get to the major areas of importance to the reader. It is therefore geared to people wanting to open a business, or to those presently operating a business, or the students learning the business in secondary schools, vocational schools, private schools, colleges, etc. The book can be a single purpose offering to anyone, or it can be part of a school's major course of study; either way the material in the book will be a reference source to the reader for many years to come.

Every year thousands of people in all walks of life quit their jobs and go into a business for themselves. Why do many fail? Not for lack of a good idea or concept. They fail mainly because they lack basic business skills, such as marketing, financing, and management ability.

People make the same basic errors.

1. Inability to organize.
2. Unable to project personal and family needs until the business is established.
3. Not knowledgeable about what equipment or service will make a business operate more efficiently.
4. Failure to anticipate expenses, such as advertising, permits, insurance, etc.

Today, there is a continuing growth in the number of people opening all types of food service business. There is no magic formula, no set standard; your idea may be a terrific idea if it is properly considered, executed, supervised, and controlled. Another big trend today in food service is the offering of courses in cooking schools, management schools; all types of training that relate to the food service industry are taking place throughout the country. Be ready to work long hours. Remember the so-called requirements for a genius are 1 percent inspiration, 99 percent perspiration. You have to make demands and impose restrictions on yourself. It is important to remember that in a business your sales come in slowly compared to the regular bills which come in on time like clockwork.

I strongly urge you to be clear about your endeavor; learn all you can. You have got to like what you are doing to be successful, but always remember the wonderful feeling of being your own successful boss. Getting ready to go into a business or a vocation is like going into battle. First get all the information and knowledge you need. Then keep your eyes, mind and attitude open.

TODAY'S BUSINESS VERSUS YESTERYEAR'S BUSINESS

It is true that at one time everything was inexpensive—labor, food, material, taxes, etc. Today nothing is inexpensive. Everything is priced high and from all indications is going higher.

COMPETITION

Competition is good. It encourages everyone to do their very best.
For example: The eating out ratio in New Orleans and in San
Francisco is very high and the caliber of restaurants is excellent.
This means that each owner must do his/her very best to stay in
business—and they do.

REASONS THAT OWNERS/MANAGERS GET INTO TROUBLE

1. Can't manage themselves or their employees.
2. Are easily discouraged when conditions get tough.
3. Have a poor attitude and fail to ask for advice.
4. Are so tied up in the day-to-day survival of the business
   that they cannot fully analyze the problems at hand.
5. Financial understanding of business is very limited.
6. Do not know, or have not traveled, in the food service
   industry.
7. They allow help to choose their own work habits and allow
   inventories to get out of control.
8. Start off without enough capital.
9. Begin the business with the wrong partner, wrong equipment layout or a poor menu.
10. Do not follow through after they issue directions to staff.
    It doesn't take employees long to realize this.

RAY PETTERUTO

Contents

How to Open and Operate a Restaurant

A Step-by-Step Guide to Financial Success

1

Introduction to the Restaurant Business

Take a moment and imagine yourself as the owner of a restaurant. What does it look like? What type of food is being served? What are the customers saying? Where are you in this picture? Where is your family? What is your weekly paycheck?

These are important questions to consider since they will help you decide whether or not the restaurant business is for you, and if it is, what type of restaurant you should open.

YOU WILL BE WORKING WITH PEOPLE AT ALL LEVELS

Because restaurant owners are constantly interacting with customers and employees they have to like people enough to cater to their likes and dislikes, and to be able to feel genuine satisfaction when they see customers enjoying a meal. They have to like people enough to pay attention to the little things that make a customer feel welcome, well-treated and anxious to return. Employees have to be carefully trained and their needs, as well as those of the customers, have to be considered.

WHAT DOES BEING YOUR OWN BOSS MEAN?

As owner/operator you can expect to be working long hours. You will reap the profits, but you will have all of the headaches too. Instead of knowing just one job you will have to know how to perform all of the jobs in the restaurant. You must train people and be able to fill in for them when they are out. You must also consider what would happen if you should become ill. Who would run the business?

Do you have, or can you acquire, a working knowledge of accounting and purchasing methods? Many restaurants fail because the owners do not keep accurate financial records. Since the average profit per meal is between 8 and 10 percent, every sale counts, and haphazard record keeping may mean disaster.

This manual will explain how you can set up a plan for record keeping and purchasing that will enable you to keep careful daily watch over the financial success of your restaurant.

ARE YOU WILLING TO LEARN FROM OTHERS WHO WANT TO HELP YOU SUCCEED?

A quick glance at the subjects covered by this manual will give you an idea of the complex job you will be undertaking. Success in this business is no accident, and a well-informed restaurant owner makes all the difference between success and failure. There are many who can help you—food service consultants, bankers, lawyers, insurance agents, equipment manufacturers, educators and government agencies.

SET UP SOME HARD AND FAST RULES TO GUIDE YOU

Set a goal that is within your reach. True, you may want to own or manage a huge deluxe food service operation, but how do you attain it? The answer is by striving for it and having faith in it. Do not get discouraged. You have got to appreciate the fact that everyone loves good food and beverages, cleanliness, service, value, and pleasant surroundings. And your faith will be rewarded by customers who return to you time and time again seeking these things. Discouragement in the food service business takes on many forms, i.e., you plan to take a day off and two of your helpers call in sick; you plan a big meal and your stove breaks down. Then there are the many critics who will tell you what is wrong.

In all of this you are the person who, as owner/operator, must have perseverance. Because if you don't show people that you have the ability to stick to the job on hand, it will affect all the help in a negative way. Don't let people talk you out of an idea. Plan your work and work your plan. Be resourceful enough to overcome problems. If, for example, two people quit in one day, apply immediate action; initially, by thinking positively, calling employment agencies, speaking to salespeople and your other helpers in an effort to replace the employees. Drive hard until you have obtained your objective—in this case, replacing these two people. Sometimes, when we quit short of a goal, success was right around the corner, but we stopped too soon.

Your health is of primary importance. Take care of it. You will more likely than not be exposed to long hours, standing, walking, etc. Have a regular physical checkup, eat the right foods. We all hear and say this, but we don't take the time to really absorb its true meaning until sometimes it is too late. Many successful manager/owners have had businesses that have had to close or be sold at a loss because the main ingredient, the owner/operator, suddenly took ill or died. The time to take care of yourself is when you are healthy.

Always be prepared to look at two sides of a future plan or present idea. Ask the questions most people avoid. Play the devil's advocate for your ideas. First admit to yourself the things you don't know, and then learn them, either through schooling or working at a job initially. You must consider taking courses in such subjects as accounting, bookkeeping, and management.

Two most important skills an owner/operator must possess are technical skills and management skills. He/she must also have the ability to do the following:

- Plan menus
- Control inventories
- Promote the business
- Attract and satisfy customers
- Supervise and motivate personnel
- Keep expenses down
- Show a profit
- Be ready and willing to work a 10 to 16 hour day, 7 days a week, if need be.

SUMMARY: First ask yourself: "Is this my cup of tea?" If you can answer truthfully that it is, then get your training by taking a job somewhere in the business with a reputable company and learn as much as you can. When you feel competent—*do your own thing!* Good Luck.

QUESTIONS

1. List six rules given in this chapter to guide you as the owner of a restaurant.

2. What are three questions you should ask yourself when considering opening a restaurant?

3. As owner-operator of a restaurant you will have to work long hours.

    True ____   False ____

4. It is not important for you as owner-operator to know how to perform all jobs in the restaurant.

    True ____   False ____

5. What is the average profit percentage per meal?

6. What is one way for you to get training before opening your restaurant?

2

What Type of Restaurant Should You Open

Restaurant styles are as varied as food itself. By 1980 it is estimated that possibly as much as half the U.S. population will be eating meals away from home for convenience, economy or recreation. You can be as creative as you like, and if your idea strikes a responsive chord in your customers they will return—and you will be on your way to success.

The following list of successful restaurant types may give you some ideas with which to form your own restaurant concept.

PLUSH TABLE SERVICE

This type of business is usually opened by an experienced chef with managerial ability, either on a one-person basis, or with a partner. One partner manages the front of the house, the other the kitchen. If neither partner is experienced in the management and structure of this type of restaurant, the complexity of preparation of food, ordering of supplies, and storage can present problems.

Menu: Varied—appeals to a large group of people.
Food cost: High.
Check average: High—serving liquor raises profits.
Staff: Cooks and service personnel must be well trained because customers will be demanding, and rightly so.
Equipment: Special equipment needed to offer this type of menu.

Design: A large building is necessary to produce the
                     volume of customers needed to support this
                     business. A "special function" room for parties
                     and weddings can raise sales.

ETHNIC RESTAURANT

The ethnic restaurant features one type of cooking such as Chinese,
French, German, etc. It can be rewarding if the owner/operator
is well versed in the particular type of food, as well as the cus-
toms and traditions of the country as they relate to the cooking and serving of food.   Ethnic restaurants are usually well
attended.

Menu: Limited to one ethnic style.
Food cost: May be low.
Check average: Good.
Type of service: Table service is the usual seating arrangement,
                   but takeout service may be available as well.
Staff: Usually only a small staff is needed because of
                   the limited menu.
Decor: May match the ethnic theme. You can use your
                   imagination and produce a unique atmosphere.

SPECIALTY HOUSE

The specialty house is usually an informal business. It can be a
hamburger stand, pancake house, doughnut shop or any one of a
great variety of specialties. This type of restaurant is especially
popular with the young customer.

Menu: Limited to one type of item that is the main
                   attraction.
Check average: Good.
Type of service: The seating can be a mixture of counter and
                   tables in a variety of designs. Takeout sections
                   are popular as are special arrangements such
                   as salad bars.
Staff: A small staff is needed. A high rate of individual
                   productivity can be gained from the employees.

Equipment: Huge equipment companies are working closely
                with food manufacturers today to produce
                specialized equipment. Your major food item
                can be well matched to special equipment that
                will improve the product. This, in turn, con-
                tributes to a more satisfied customer.

CAFETERIA

Line Cafeteria

This is the most popular type of cafeteria. The line of customers
passes along the displayed food, making selections and paying the
cashier at the end of the line. Items such as sandwiches, salads,
desserts and beverages may be picked up by the customer; an ex-
ception may be the main entrees.

Scramble-up Cafeteria

Each customer walks directly to the desired item and serves him/
herself.

Kitchen: Most of the cooking can be done beforehand in
                a separate kitchen area. It is a good idea for the
                person who cooks to serve, so he/she may relate
                to the customers and hear their comments on
                the food and service.

Design: Usually station ropes are needed to control the
                traffic. Heading signs direct the customer to
                each food choice.

Location: Cafeterias do well in factories, schools, sta-
                diums and stores; however, the outlook on
                cafeterias as freestanding units is poor, with
                some exceptions.

COFFEE SHOP

A person who wants to do little cooking and knows how to relate
well to people, can be extremely successful operating a coffee

shop.   His/her personal input can be instrumental in cutting the cost of the operation.

Menu:	Varied, with a large number of choices.
Food cost:	High.
Type of service:	Varies from counter service to booth or table service. A profitable takeout service can also be developed.
Staff:	Labor cost is high.
Decor:	An informal look with a bright cheerful atmosphere.

WALK-UP SERVICE

The key to success in a self-service operation is to locate in a busy area.   Then management must address itself to quick, clean service techniques.

Menu:	A small variety of items.
Check average:	Low—quick customer turnover is necessary.
Type of service:	Customers wait in line and give their orders to the clerk. Drinks, utensils and napkins are selected separately.
Staff:	Small—each person has a specific task to perform. There are no behind-the-scene people.
Kitchen:	An active production kitchen near the main customer service area (front of the house).
Packaging:	The major menu item (fish, steak, hamburger) is usually precooked and packaged to insure freshness and quality. Packaging is important because much of this business is takeout and the product should be just as good at its final destination as it was when it left the restaurant.
Design:	The seating arrangement is usually tight, and customers share tables—which promotes a quick turnover. Additional seating outdoors will usually attract customers.
Decor:	The menu is usually mounted on the wall with professional photographs. No homemade signs should be used.

DRIVE-IN

Drive-ins have been popular for many years. Chain companies have made their mark in this field. The initial cost for real estate, design, exterior and construction is high. In some cases, an owner of land may build a drive-in and lease it to another person who will manage it.

The best route to take is the same one the chain companies take, but on a smaller scale. Being the owner *and* operator in the beginning can make the difference between success and failure. Being an owner/operator in the beginning will take you into the nitty gritty problem areas you must face and conquer. You cannot afford the luxury of hiring a manager and then later finding out he/she is not a luxury but a liability. You will be learning by doing and growing in your position.

FAST FOOD

Many franchise companies are in the fast-food business. Strict management formulas, menu control, a particular style of architecture and much advertising have helped these businesses become successful. Fast-food operations have multiplied via the franchise route; however, an individual can do well on a small basis. This market, though it can be difficult to get into can be a profitable self-operated business.

Menu:	Standardized.
Type of service:	As a rule most food is carried out of the building.
Location:	Can operate in all settings—city, suburb or country.
Advertising:	A certain advertising budget must be established.

LUNCHEONETTE

Although the check average is usually low, this type of business can be profitable to the owner/operator.

Menu:	Varied with a large number of choices; "Daily Specials" of hot foods, desserts and seasonal dishes are popular and successful.
Type of service:	Quick service, cleanliness and speedy take-out service are essential.

Kitchen: Cooking is usually done in a remote kitchen.
Location: Usually located in department stores, offices or factories.

OTHER FOOD OUTLETS TO COI.'SIDER

Catering
Restaurant Stands
Hotel Concessions
Taverns and Bars
Vending Machines
Airline Catering
Steamship Concessions
Railroad Catering
Delicatessens
Bakeries
Camps
Theater Restaurants

The businesses mentioned in this chapter show the wide variety of possibilities for successful food service management. When making your choice of business it is important to remember that any food offering can be varied. There is no single or magic formula you must adhere to.

If you have what you feel is a different concept, do not necessarily discard it because it has never been done before. Think it out, plan it out, and talk to knowledgeable people in the field in question. Once your decision is made, stick to it and work hard. Common sense and good business ethics will help you succeed. *You* are the only one who can make it happen.

MAGIC FORMULA FOR SUCCESS

If there were a magic formula for success it would probably be stated as follows:

1. Decide on the type or kind of customer you wish to serve.
2. Develop a blueprint (the menu) for that market.
3. Develop the restaurant around the menu in decor, advertising, equipment, service, etc.

4. Locate the business in the economic area you feel will support it.
5. Merchandise your restaurant in color, style, etc.
6. Be ready to change as times change, in menu, building appearance, customers' likes and dislikes, etc.
7. Insist on *good food, service, courtsey, value.* Be people oriented.

Think Big

It's good to think big but be reasonable and realistic.

QUESTIONS

1. Name eight different types of restaurants mentioned in the chapter.

2. Name six other food outlets mentioned.

3. The check average in a luncheonette is usually high.

    True ____   False ____

4. Ethnic restaurants usually specialize in one type of cooking.

    True ____   False ____

5. Managing a restaurant having plush table service does not require much experience.

    True ____   False ____

6. What is the difference between a cafeteria and walk-up service?

7. What two things will help you succeed?

3
Location

A good restaurant location is one that is easy for its customers to get to, has ample parking for the volume of business you hope to do, looks good (compared to the competition), does not have a negative image to overcome and is in an area where property is appreciating in value rather than depreciating. Let us consider each of these important points.

WHO ARE YOUR CUSTOMERS?

Are your customers people who will come on foot, or will they drive? Will they want speedy service, or a more leisurely type of atmosphere? Do they earn $15,000 a year of $5,000? When sizing up a location, talk to your potential customers. One way is to politely stop people on the street and openly talk to them about your ideas. You may be pleasantly surprised by the good suggestions you may get. Talk to other merchants in the area—the neighbors, bankers, salespeople, store clerks—listen to their ideas on your proposed menu and location.

If you are considering buying an already existing restaurant, you must not assume that you will inherit the previous owner's customers. The previous owner had his/her own friends and catered to their needs. The customers responded by patronizing his/her restaurant. You will also have to cultivate your own group of steady customers.

ACCESSIBILITY

Once you have identified your customers, you must make it as convenient as possible for them to patronize your restaurant. An inner-city location with limited parking facilities may do well if there is sufficient pedestrian traffic in the immediate neighborhood, and if your menu appeals to those who are walking by.

On the other hand, a parking lot should be well lighted with adequate approach and exit areas. If you are in an area where winter snow is likely to be a problem you will need to make arrangements for snow removal well in advance of the winter season. Always try to project by asking yourself if the parking lot can be expanded in the future.

If your restaurant is located on a busy road or highway it is important that the signs are big enough to see, and the driveway wide enough so customers driving by will be able to safely slow down and make the turn. This rule applies to all restaurants, although it is particularly important for drive-ins.

YOUR COMPETITION

Take a good look at the competition in the area you are considering for a location. Ask yourself the questions, "How good is their equipment, personnel, building structure, interior and exterior design, menu, parking facilities, etc. compared to what I would have? Who would customers find more likable, my competition or me and why would they prefer one over the other?"

If you are thinking of specializing in hamburgers in an area where some of the larger hamburger chains are already represented you must realize the magnitude of your competition. They have the resources to advertise heavily, are well managed, and will be strong competition for you. This does not mean, however, that your hamburger operation could not succeed. It certainly can if you have a well-run business. As an independent restaurant owner you can provide the personal touch that the larger companies can never imitate.

HISTORY

It is important to check out the restaurant history of the areas you are considering. Certain types of restaurants and areas may not take to each other.   If you are planning to open a pizza parlor and you know that six people tried in a particular area and were unsuccessful before you, then you know pizza is a poor risk for this location. This holds true for other specialty restaurants—pancake houses, roast beef hearths, etc. They just do not do well in some locations.

GROWTH FACTOR

Consider the economy of the area—is this a neighborhood where property values are declining or can you look forward to your investment increasing in value year by year?   The hard-working restaurant owner wants to see his/her investment grow, and to locate in a deteriorating area may work against this.

Based on the type of trade in the area, how much sales volume could you realistically expect? Would the sales volume be enough to cover your expenses and give you a profit? If the answer is no, continue looking for a more suitable location.

CITY VERSUS SUBURBAN LOCATION

The difficulties faced by city locations—crime, transportation, parking, high rents, to name a few—have led to the increasing popularity of suburban locations. These are frequently located near malls and shopping areas and have plenty of parking space. Although suburban locations may do very little breakfast business, the lunch and dinner trade is usually abundant.

Let us next consider some of the ways of buying into a chosen location, either by buying an existing restaurant, buying a closed restaurant, building a freestanding restaurant, or by leasing.

BUYING AN EXISTING RESTAURANT

An established restaurant that seems to be in a good location but is operating unprofitably may only need some changes in menu, and better financial controls and followups in order for the tide to turn.

CLOSED RESTAURANT

Do not invest money in a restaurant that has closed until you have a clear picture of why it closed. As stated before, some types of restaurants do not do well in certain areas. If this is the case, you would be wise not to follow in the previous owner's footsteps. If the reason for closing was poor food or poor service, customers may still regard the restaurant as taboo and, unless you can drastically change the image and offer better quality and service, you should probably avoid buying it.

BUILDING A FREE-STANDING RESTAURANT

The main advantage to building your own structure is that you can design and lay out your plans according to your own specifications. Since a restaurant is designed around its menu, building your own restaurant can save you the problems of extensive remodeling which might be required if you bought an existing restaurant. You can be sure that fixtures, equipment, food storage, preparation and dining areas are all arranged as you want them.

You should have the building done by a reputable contracting firm if you have no prior knowledge of the construction trade. You should get estimates for the work to be done from several contractors. Check out their reputations and credit rating. Ask for names of earlier customers and see if they were satisfied. This will relieve you of the worries of dealing with plumbers, tradespeople, builders, etc. and will assure you that all federal, state and city zoning requirements and building codes will be satisfied.

Successful restaurant owners must be quick to adapt their own personal concepts to those of their customers as regards likes, dislikes and eating preferences. This means that in building your own restaurant it is wise to have an alternative plan in mind should you want to use the building for a different type of food service at a later date.

LEASING

In some cases locations can be leased with the owner of the property building to your specifications, and agreeing to a long-term lease with options set up by you, your attorney and the owner. You should be sure before you sign that the owner will allow you to change your restaurant concept if you so desire.

There are cases where you can lease for an agreed percentage of sales depending on who puts up the building and equipment. One example would be if an investor erects the building and equips it for a percent of your sales.

Be careful when considering leasing an already equipped restaurant. Unless the present operator is running a successful business and is willing to stay with you and effect an easy changeover, this can be like opening a business that has already failed.

WHEN A LOCATION IS FOR SALE

Ask yourself these questions:

1. How long has it been for sale?
2. Have you or anyone you know eaten there?
3. Are all the necessary utilities available? (220 electrical line, dishwasher, etc.)
4. Does the location have gas, water, electricity, sewerage, garbage pickup, etc.? Who pays for these services?
5. How does the present equipment fit your menu?
6. What does the rent include?
7. Who pays for any needed improvements?
8. Why does the owner want to sell?
9. Who pays for repairs and maintenance?
10. Is the business making a profit? Can you go in and also make a profit? Did the owner make a profit by being owner, cook, manager, waiter/waitress and dishroom attendant? Did they work many, many hours a week to make this profit? As the new owner would you have to do the same thing?
11. Who was the owner before the present one? Talk to both of them and see if they can tell you anything that will help you make your decision.
12. Get the sales figures and have them verified by an auditor.
13. How is the owner of the property? Cooperative, fair, difficult to deal with?
14. Is there a liquor license? Can one be obtained if there is none?
15. Is the area changing for the better or the worse?

16. What would the present owner change or leave alone if he/she decided to stay?
17. Ask about existing physical problems; for example, plumbing, wiring, alleyway to make rear-door delivery.

SUMMARY: When you have found what you think is the right location, study it from all angles. Listen to real estate salespeople but don't be easily oversold or too quick to say yes. Is the restaurant in an area that is growing? What industries are in the area? Will they add to or detract from your concept and location? What do you feel is the success factor? Are the economic conditions in the area stable? Deteriorating? Flourishing? What is the national economic trend? The industry trend? Have you sufficient personal finances?

Many graphs, charts, formulas can be administered to grade a location, i.e., the use of a traffic study. This should give you an idea of how you will draw customers. There has been a trend in recent years toward the average volume of business increasing with store size. Also, one has to be willing to extend oneself more financially for good locations, plus a greater dollar commitment to inventory, fixtures, and personnel. Four out of five locations surveyed by so-called research experts are rejected.

Seek out all agencies that can give you helpful data, such as:

• Real estate agency
• Small Business Administration
• Department of Commerce
• Local Chamber of Commerce
• Your lawyer, accountant, banker, insurance agent, and restaurant consultant

Be thoroughly informed, collect all the facts before you act.

Things to consider on an A, B, C, D basis.

A B C D
☐ ☐ ☐ ☐   Size of your city's trading area.
☐ ☐ ☐ ☐   The success of competition.
☐ ☐ ☐ ☐   The total purchasing power of the area.
☐ ☐ ☐ ☐   How the monies are distributed.
☐ ☐ ☐ ☐   The size and number and quality of competition.
☐ ☐ ☐ ☐   General appearance of the area.

☐ ☐ ☐ ☐   Direction of area growth.
☐ ☐ ☐ ☐   How rigid are zoning laws?
☐ ☐ ☐ ☐   Condition of roads to your business.
☐ ☐ ☐ ☐   Complementary worth of adjacent stores.
☐ ☐ ☐ ☐   Parking.
☐ ☐ ☐ ☐   Area vulnerability to unpleasant competition.
☐ ☐ ☐ ☐   Cost of site.
☐ ☐ ☐ ☐   Foot traffic.
☐ ☐ ☐ ☐   Automobile traffic count.
☐ ☐ ☐ ☐   Quality of available labor.
☐ ☐ ☐ ☐   Labor rates of pay.
☐ ☐ ☐ ☐   Expansion possibilities.
☐ ☐ ☐ ☐   Taxation burden.
☐ ☐ ☐ ☐   Quality of fire/police protection.
☐ ☐ ☐ ☐   Schools, cultural, community atmosphere.
☐ ☐ ☐ ☐   Projected quality of location in 10 years.
☐ ☐ ☐ ☐   Availability of all utilities.

QUESTIONS

1.   What are five important steps to consider in choosing a restaurant location?

2.   List three reasons why restaurants in city locations may have problems.

3.   When a restaurant is for sale what are some of the questions that should be asked?

4.   The history of the area where the restaurant is located is not as important as how well the business is run.

    True ____   False ____

5.   What is the main advantage of erecting your own building?

6.   An inner-city restaurant must have a large parking lot.

    True ____   False ____

7.   There is a good chance of an investment increasing in value in an area where property values are declining.

    True ____   False ____

4
The Franchise Route

Buying or leasing a franchise would seem to be the safest and simplest way for an inexperienced person to enter the restaurant business. In many cases this is true, but a closer look at the pros and cons of franchises may help you decide whether this route is for you.

THE COMPANY NAME

The big food service chains have spent millions of dollars researching consumer tastes and promoting this knowledge to create a restaurant experience with the broadest possible appeal. Customers will come to you because they already know and like the products.

On the other hand, all that money invested in maintaining the company image means that you are not free to change the menu, style of cooking, architecture or management. This can lead to problems since the typical restaurant owner is an independent soul who goes into the business because he/she wants to do things his/her way!

TRAINING

The training of franchise owners can be as streamlined as the making of a hamburger. You can expect to be trained either at a company school or at another franchise. This can be a definite advantage to the inexperienced owner.

ORDERING, PURCHASING AND FINANCIAL CONTROLS

The big companies have all aspects of their business down to a science and because of the sheer volume of their purchasing power can obtain food and other supplies at the lowest possible cost. Individual owners who wish to order supplies elsewhere may find it difficult to compete against this.

Banks and large equipment companies tend to feel easier when they see the name of a well-known franchise. They know that a large, well-established chain increases the chances of success (repayment of the loan) and that the large franchises have the financial resources to endure a lean season of business when an individual owner/operator sometimes cannot.

Not all franchises have a good name in the banking and financial community. Your banker will be able to tell you whether or not the franchise you are considering is a good business risk. Listen to his/her advice.

Because franchisors vary so in cost, quality of services provided, business ethics and type of contract, you and your lawyer will want to investigate the following areas:

1. Find out all you can about the company. Write to all state and federal administrative offices such as the Small Business Administration, local Chamber of Commerce, Better Business Bureau, State Department of Commerce, etc. to learn all you can about the company.

2. Get the names of all the officers of the company that is trying to sell you the franchise. Have your attorney run a check on them and on the financial position of the company.

3. How long has the company been franchising?

4. What is the track record of the company locally and nationally?

5. Who is the nearest franchisee? Get his/her name and address and talk with him/her. Ask all the questions your advisors and you may have.

6. Get a copy of the contract you will have to sign and bring it to your attorney for his/her opinion.

7. How experienced are the principals of the company with the food service product?

8. Where there any failures?

9. What are the future plans of the company? Do they have the capital and the people to expand?

10. What training, followup and site selection will the franchisor undertake?

11. Who pays for the paper supplies, and small supplies such as pots and pans?

12. What about advertising charges, or the ability to buy products from companies of your choice?

13. Can you equip your business with workable, used equipment, or will they insist on new equipment?

14. What would you do if equipment breaks down or there is a power failure? Is a supplementary generator included as standard equipment?

15. Who pays for menu printing?

16. Who pays for outdoor signs? Who pays for maintenance of outdoor signs?

17. How are other franchisees doing with this company?

18. Do you have a specific area assured to you? Consult your attorney.

19. Be certain your attorney does a thorough job of checking out royalty charges, length of contract, fixed charges, quotas, purchasing requirements (if any), arbitration privileges and any other matters regarding your contract that he/she considers important.

20. Can you sign the contract as a corporation officer, or must you sign with a personal signature?

21. What is the cost of the franchise? How can it be financed?

22. How much can you earn?

23. If you need special qualifications, who will train you after the opening?

24. Is the franchise product a passing fancy—one that will become obsolete in 5 to 10 years?

25. If you want to terminate the contract, how can this be done?

26. If the company wants to terminate you, how can they do it?

SUMMARY: Franchising is a way of life for companies, enhancing the sales of their product while spreading the fame of the company name. It is a good way for a person without special skills to be trained in every aspect of the restaurant business. Be certain you check all the facts closely. Retain a knowledgeable attorney to give you advice and counsel. Also, be sure you can adapt to the type of franchise you are intending to enter.

QUESTIONS

1. When you buy into a franchise you can usually change or add to the menu if you so desire.

    True ___   False ___

2. What are four advantages of buying or leasing a franchise?

3. Where can you get franchise information?

4. Banks and financial institutions always look favorably on applications for a franchise.

    True ___   False ___

5. Why would you want to investigate before buying or leasing a franchise?

5
How Much Cash
Do You Need?

The type of restaurant you get into will determine the amount of money you need. However, the well-planned and well-financed restaurant with ample *reserve* for *expected* expenses, as well as for those which are *unexpected*, has a far greater chance of success than the *ill-equipped, "shoestring" operation,* which forces the owner to work 24 hours a day in order to show a profit. Your banker, lawyer and accountant are the people who will help you arrive at a realistic estimate of how much money you will need to borrow to start out right. In order to benefit from their advice, you must be prepared to openly discuss with them your anticipated income, your expenses, and how and when your debts will be paid. This chapter will describe some of the major expenses involved, and will alert you to other factors which must be considered in deciding how much money is needed to open a restaurant.

THE BUILDING

Whether you buy an existing restaurant or build a new one, you will need to convince your banker that you are a good credit risk. Chances are good that your loan will be approved if you have already proven yourself successful in another business venture. If you are buying into a well-established franchise, the good name of the company will help toward getting your loan approved. Your banker will help you decide what type of loan will be best for you, but avoid the habit of frequent, short-term borrowing.

Leasing a profitable restaurant that already exists, or has been built to your specifications, may be a less expensive way for you to begin, particularly if it contains the equipment you will need. You will then be paying the owner either a monthly fee or an agreed upon percentage of your gross sales. In this case you will need to borrow enough cash to be sure you can meet your monthly expenses until the restaurant is firmly established and paying for itself.

EQUIPMENT

Great care should be exercised in selecting the right equipment for your restaurant. It is possible to lease equipment, buy it outright, or buy it on time. If you decide on the third method, you must remember that equipment dealers usually want a 30 to 35 percent down payment. In some cases they can afford to be liberal in making financial arrangements since they usually own the title to the equipment until it is fully paid for. This means they can repossess your equipment if you fail to meet your payments, so be sure to allow enough cash in your total borrowing plan to cover such payments.

RESTAURANT SUPPLIERS, FOOD SUPPLIERS, VENDORS

These companies may offer you a discount if you are able to pay for the merchandise sooner than the normal 30 to 60 days, but you will have to determine whether you actually will be able to do so. At the beginning paying bills is difficult.

BUILD A RESERVE

Start with reserve capital and continue to build it year after year. Many restaurants fail because the owners did not have the resources to deal with the unexpected. Ask yourself how much you will need from the business to live the first year, and then plan accordingly.

Bankers, lawyers, accountants and consultants can help a great deal; however, you must make them part of your problem-solving. Don't just take advice from them, but let them spell out exactly what they mean to do for you.

Apart from checking on you, your references, your location and your concept, the main concern of anyone lending you money (be it banks, friends or any other source) is your ability to repay it. There are two types of loans available for raising capital:

Long-term Borrowing

A long-term loan is for money you don't expect to pay back right away. It is usually borrowed for a period of more than one year. (It is possible that the person selling the business will hold a mortgage note.)

Short-term Borrowing

Short-term borrowing is for money borrowed for a year or less to help in an emergency, but not to pay an expense such as rent, because the bank views rent as something that the owner/operator has to have each and every month and does not regard it as a short-term emergency.

Always be prepared for the unexpected and have a reliable plan in case of urgent money needs.

COLLATERAL

A bank or other lending institution wants to be certain that the money they loan to you is secured, and you may be asked to post collateral to insure this. There are many forms of collateral, for example, a person who is in a good financial position may sign on your behalf to enable you to get the loan, by posting real estate, bonds, insurance policies, etc., all of which can be offered as security. Or if you yourself have any or all of these, you can post them yourself. This only occurs when, in the lender's opinion, you have not yet reached a point where you are considered financially strong enough for the bank to give you the loan without asking for collateral of some type. Once your balance sheets, and profit and loss statements have developed a trend for profitability, your signature alone will be sufficient.

SOURCES FOR LOANS

Let us discuss where you can borrow money. Some possible sources are friends, relatives, food and equipment dealers, manufacturers, partners, The Small Business Administration, banks, insurance companies, other business people. Remember, no matter who lends you the money, the most important thing is how it is going to be paid back.

Whether you want to borrow money from a bank, a corporation or an individual, go about it in a formal, businesslike fashion. First, appreciate that banks in particular have had bad experiences with restaurants. Whoever the prospective lender may be, make your approach to them with care. Have your accountant prepare a profit and loss statement. A balance sheet (sample shown on page 28) will show the prospective lender that you know the importance of profit and loss statements in order to insure a profit. You should know about these documents and how to control expenses before they happen—also how to calculate cash flow in a business.

THE BALANCE SHEET

The main function of a balance sheet is to keep you aware of how your business is doing. Your profit and loss statement and balance sheet, properly taken care of, are the two most important documents you must learn how to control, project and analyze in your business. Consider also the person lending you the money. If he/she knows you have studied and learned from a manual, such as this, and you go to see him/her with a presentation that includes: (1) why you want the money; (2) a history of your background; and (3) your financial statements, all of these will help you secure the loan, because banks and individuals lending money want assurance that they are dealing with good business people.

What else will you need money for?

1. Your personal living expenses until such time as the business can support you;
2. Equipment, food supplies, lease deposits, utilities, consultant fees, insurances, payroll, telephone, remodeling, advertising;

3. One thought on cash needs; I feel you should have enough cash reserve to carry your personal needs and the restaurant for the first year.

SUMMARY: Cash is something you never seem to have enough of, especially when starting a business. My suggestion would be to start small. True, it is nice to have all new equipment, but if you start off with good workable, used equipment, you can save probably 50 to 60 percent of what new equipment would cost you. One example of when you should buy new equipment is if you are going to open a business that will operate 24 hours a day, 7 days a week, especially equipment with motors. One example of when you could buy good used equipment is for the purchase of stainless steel work tables, storage racks, etc. These, even if used, are always a savings if they function for your needs.

Be sure to watch the percentage of interest you agree to pay on money you borrow. Compare interest rates before signing, because 1 to 2 percent saving over a long period of time can be very beneficial to your success. Also compare the insurance coverage offered by several different companies. Do not just agree to bring in a company service or product—first understand fully what is being offered, find out the cost and then compare with the terms or products of other companies.

Talk to others in the restaurant business. What has been their experience in borrowing money to open a business? What would they advise you to do or not to do.

For a person going into a business, I would recommend a financial background as follows:

1. Have what monies you need to live on for approximately one year, either in savings or through another family member working, so that you can sustain yourself until the business starts paying off.

2. Always have a slush account, or monies set aside for the unexpected. By slush account is meant a source of funds always on hand.

BALANCE SHEET

A Balance Sheet is a statement of a company's findings of its financial picture on a particular day of the year. As of that moment it provides a complete picture of what the firm owns and owes, and its net worth—as illustrated in the example shown below.

Consolidated Balance Sheet, as of December 31
($000 omitted):

Assets	1976	1975
Cash, etc	44,421	37,429
Sh. tm. invest	71,714	65,152
Receiv., net	32,239	27,828
(2) Inventories	11,117	9,684
Prepay., etc	16,677	16,289
Total curr	176,168	156,382
(1) Net prop., net	1,015,590	844,619
Oth. assets, etc	59,039	45,982
Intangibles	33,370	30,781
Total	1,284,167	1,077,764
Liabilities:		
Notes, etc. pay	30,361	23,885
Accts. etc. pay	100,651	83,694
Income tax	40,048	32,338
Total curr	171,060	139,917
Lg. tm. debt	496,548	446,319
Def. inc. tax	50,919	38,685
Secur. depos	40,246	35,635

To give one example of the approximate amount of money needed to open a business; a restaurant seating 175 people, and specializing in roast beef sandwiches would need approximately $75,000. This is for a business in a rented location. You can easily appreciate the big dollar investment it takes to start a business. Again, it depends on the type of business you open, because that will vary the opening dollar cost.

QUESTIONS

1. A cash reserve is not as vital to the food service business as it is to some other types of business.

    True ____   False ____

2. A long-term loan is money borrowed for a period of more than one year.

    True ____   False ____

3. Equipment dealers, in most cases, will accept 5 to 10 percent as a down payment on equipment purchases.

    True ____   False ____

4. What is the main function of a balance sheet?

5. You will need money for food and equipment. For what other things will money be needed?

6. Explain collateral.

7. How much cash reserve should you have?

6
Menu

The menu is the blueprint of your restaurant and has many functions: it attracts and intrigues the customer; it provides you with a guide for ordering, purchasing and estimating income; it determines the layout of the kitchen and the special equipment you will need; it sets the tone of your restaurant—formal, ethnic, or whatever the case may be—which will help you furnish and decorate it appropriately.

Customers like to be *surprised* with different food offerings, but they also very much like the *security* of knowing they can always order again something they have eaten and enjoyed before. For this reason, most menus have three parts:

1. The formally printed menu with food listed according to price range and type.
2. The flier—a mimeographed insert describing the daily specials.
3. The rider—a small piece of paper clipped to the regular menu describing one or two inexpensive items, leftovers from the previous day's special.

The printed menu changes seasonally as different foods become available. The fliers change on a 30- to 60-day cycle, although in some restaurants they change daily.

TRUTH IN MENU (WHAT IS IT?)

The food service industry for many years has had a small segment that misrepresent items on a menu. For example: *Veal Cutlets* were advertised but a veal patty was served. *Chicken Salad* was advertised but turkey meat was used. *Whipped Cream* was advertised but substitutes were used. This misrepresentation in some areas of the food service industry has been widespread and laws are presently in effect protecting the customer from false advertising on menus. It would be harmful to your business if you were to be fined and named in a newspaper as a violator of these laws.

The purpose of a menu is to sell food—your food. Daily Specials, Businessmen's Luncheons, Morning Specials, Season Specials and Area Specials all are pluses that make your menu sell your products. Whenever possible use plentiful and economical foods. Feature the in-season product.

Seek advice from a printing house as to the design, type of print and position of items on the menu. More people will look at items on the right side of a two-fold menu, so the featured items should be placed there.

Prepare for price changes when designing your menu. It is important not to write in by hand the changed prices on your menu. Use overprints that can be fitted into the price section and will maintain the professional touch, while keeping the cost factor down by avoiding the necessity to reprint the entire menu.

Desserts, side dishes, soups, salads and takeout items should be promoted as an add-on source for additional sales.

Menus distributed to nearby motels, hotels, gas stations and tourist booths can give you excellent added volume and exposure.

Assist the passerby and potential customer by placing a menu in a window frame with a light focusing on it. This habit will prove beneficial, and in many cases prove to be the deciding factor on whether or not the person will come in or walk on by.

Make it your business to collect samples of menus offered by nearby competitors. Compare them with your own. You will be surprised how easy it is to find new ways to present your products, new items to feature and so on.

The menu is your image, your face, your personality. It reflects the ultimate in what you want to portray to the customers. As you greet patrons, personally hand them an open menu. A menu left on a table or counter, or in a booth does nothing to make your customer feel welcome.

The menu should spell out exactly what is offered for the price so there is no doubt in the customer's mind whether or not he/she is entitled to one potato, one vegetable, roll and butter, etc. Plate make-up should be exactly as the menu advertises it, i.e., if peas and mashed potatoes are advertised, never substitute another vegetable without the customer's approval.

Communicate with your employees. Each employee serving the customers should be aware of the available items daily, what the featured item is, and what can be offered as an alternative to unavailable items. Nothing turns a customer off more than to be told there is "no meat loaf," "no chicken," etc., without being then told what is available.

FORMULA PREPARATION

Once you have determined the cast of characters you will put on the menu, it is very important to then create a formula for each item. Let us suppose you want to feature meat loaf. First, decide on the ingredients to be used—beef base (extract), hot water, onions, potatoes, carrots, beef, eggs, bread crumbs. Make a typed list of all the ingredients required, then write down the exact steps which must be taken in making the meat loaf, the oven temperature, cooking time and the type of pan used. This is important because customers are creatures of habit, and once you have established the best possible way to produce the meat loaf, and it has been accepted by the customer, that is the way you will want to make it each and every time. If in spite of using the finest ingredients, you find your meat loaf is not selling, do some experimenting to see how you can improve it. If it is still not selling, remove it from the menu for a while and possibly try offering it again at a later date.

FOOD COST

"How do I arrive at a selling price?" is the age old question. You've heard it said about many restaurants that the price of the fancy rugs, lamps, etc. are passed on to the customer to pay. This is true. The price listed on the menu is a combination of what the food cost and what is needed in order to meet expenses and realize a profit.

The following is one standard way of calculating food cost. Suppose a 20 lb. turkey (*cooked cost* not raw cost) was $2.25 per lb. At approximately 14¢ per oz. a 3 oz. serving will cost 42¢.

3 oz. turkey	.42¢
Potato & veg.	.09
(once measured)	
Gravy & dressing	.03
(once measured)	
Roll & butter	.05
	.59¢–Total Cost
Add 10% shrinkage factor	.06
	.65¢–True Cost of Meal

Using a 3 x cost break you can arrive at selling cost as follows:

$$.65¢$$
$$x \quad 3$$
$$\$1.95–\text{Menu price of turkey plate}$$

The *food cost*, which you must now calculate for *each and every item on the menu,* will tell you what percentage of the menu price is spent solely on purchasing and preparing the food:

.65¢–Cooked cost of turkey plate.
_____   = 34% Food Cost
$1.95 = Menu Price

Your accountant can tell whether your menu prices are realistic by comparing your other expenses (rent, utilities, salaries, taxes, insurance, etc.) with your expected volume of sales.

Your menu should present a sales mix of high- and low-cost food items. A high-cost food item such as Club Steak (55%) may belong on your menu because people want it. By introducing a Delmonico Steak Special (40%) you may educate your customers to prefer the Delmonico, a saving to them and a profit to you.

The specials that you offer on the menu flier should not compete with the regular items on the printed menu; that is, the same item should not appear at an expensive and an inexpensive price.

All-American foods such as hot dogs, hamburgers, chicken, pizza, fish and french fries are all known and accepted by customers. If you include these items on your menu be sure they are of good quality. Remember that your customers know what they taste like at competitor's restaurants.

The menu of the future will reflect the changes in American eating habits. For instance, calories and nutritional content may be spelled out as customers become more diet and nutrition conscious. Stay in touch with the times. Be ready to change.

SOME RELATED MENU SALES INCREASING TIPS

1. Eye-catching window displays.
2. Hot biscuits, rolls or bread.
3. Fresh coffee made at regular intervals. Individual carafes for coffee.
4. Table decorations—a small plant or one fresh flower.
5. Special banquet menu available for showers, graduations or anniversaries.
6. Have tomorrow's menu displayed at cashier's desk and/or at exit.
7. Have doggie bags available.
8. Steak markers—paper frills for ribs—colorful stirrers for drinks.
9. Covers for hot plates—fancy doilies under fruit cups and juices.
10. Specials for quick coffee breaks.
11. Menu clip-ons for daily specials.
12. Novel place mats that are changed at regular intervals.
13. Theater tie-in, if possible.
14. Kitchen open for inspection on request.
15. Space on checks for customer's suggestions or criticisms.
16. Serve small cookies with ice cream or hot chocolate.
17. Use amber glasses to make milk look creamy.
18. Promote special salads in the summer—hot specialities in the winter.

MENU PROMOTION SUGGESTIONS

1. Table Tents—Featuring food specials, drinks, desserts.
2. A Special Night—Nationality Night, Harvest meals, etc.
3. Waitresses—Wearing special pins, hats, etc.
4. Seasonal Trimmings—Thanksgiving turkeys, Christmas holly, etc.

5. Wording—A menu item is better written as, for example "Old-Fashioned Irish Stew" rather than "Irish Stew"

GENERAL OUTLINE SUGGESTIONS

Breakfast

Dishes
Pastries

Lunch and Dinner

Hot Plate Dinner, vegetable and potato,
                    roll and butter
Meats with gravy, potatoes
Hot Vegetable Plates
Diet Menu Special (this can develop into a profitable sector of your
    business)
Salads—Sandwiches
Combo—Business Lunch
            Cup of soup or juice, entree, dessert, beverage
Takeout business
Selling homemade whole pies, cakes
Recognize special anniversaries, birthday parties, etc. with a cake.
At Thanksgiving time offer to roast whole turkeys for your customers.

PREPARATION TIPS

First thing in the morning turn on all equipment and check to be sure everything is functioning properly, and then adjust equipment dial setting so as not to waste energy.

Many items on your menu can be prepared the day before, and many last-minute problems can be eliminated by getting into this habit. If you need potatoes peeled for a stew, or tuna fish salad is featured on the luncheon menu, prepare them the day before. Once you have established the menu cycles to be used, you will be able to outline work that can be done the day before to make your operation run more efficiently.

STUDY YOUR MIX OF MENU

The following is a suggested method to use in determining the true picture of what your menu is presenting to the public. Use it for each item on the menu. Compare your results with your competitor's menus. In this way you can be your own critic of your business.

A method to use in studying your entrees as to portion sizes, costs and selling prices, is to prepare a list on which each of these elements is shown in its proper column, as follows:

Hamburger

Portion size	4 oz.
Cost	.35¢
Cost of other ingredients*	.17
Add 10%	.05
Total Cost	.57¢
Selling Price	$1.35
Percentage food cost	42.2

Meat Loaf

Portion size	4 oz.
Cost	.41¢
Cost of other ingredients**	.17
Add 10%	.06
Total Cost	.64¢
Selling Price	$1.75
Percentage food cost	36.6

*Hamburger needs roll, mustard/catsup, pickles
**Meat loaf needs potato, vegetable, roll and butter
These costs must be reflected in "other item" section.

SPECIAL NOTE

It has been proven many times that a short menu will not only be accepted better by the customer but will also insure a good profit for the operation.

People expect something special when it is noted as such on the menu. Why is it special?

MENU VARIETY

Following is a list of items that may be used as a guide in making up your daily menu.

Before you establish the variety you would like to carry on the menu, study your equipment, taking into consideration what the equipment you have can handle.

Check the number of items you can carry on the menu and then decide on the variety you can have from day to day.

Beef
Baked Noodles with Hamburger
Barbecued Meat Balls
Chicken-Fried Steak
Hamburger Steak
Indian Beef Pot Pie
Meat Balls with Spaghetti
Meat Loaf
Old-Fashioned Beef Stew
Roast Beef
Spanish Rice with Hamburger
Stuffed Green Pepper
Swiss Steak

Veal
Breaded Veal Chop
Breaded Veal Cutlet
Fricassee of Veal with Vegetables
Roast Veal (Leg)
Veal Stew with Spaghetti

Pork
Braised Pork Chops
Breaded Pork Chops
Roast Fresh Pork Ham
Spanish Ham with Potatoes
Spare Ribs with Sauerkraut

Variety Items
Braised Liver (Beef or Pork)
Baked Liver with Onions
Chili
Frankfurters with Baked Beans
Sliced Frankfurters with Spaghetti
Stuffed Frankfurters with Potatoes

Fish
Baked Halibut Steak
Baked Tuna Fish with Noodles au Gratin
Cod Fish Balls
Fillet of Fried Haddock
Fried Fish Cakes
Fried Oysters
Salmon Croquettes with sauce
Salmon Loaf with sauce

Poultry
Chicken a la King
Chicken Pot Pie
Old-Fashioned Chicken and Noodles
Roast Chicken with Dressing
Turkey Dinner

Hot Sandwiches

Beef	Pork
Ham	Turkey
Meat Loaf	Veal
(served with potatoes and gravy)	

Soups
Chicken Noodle
Lima Bean
Manhattan Clam Chowder
New England Clam Chowder
Old-Fashioned Cream of Potato
Split Pea
Vegetable

MENU GENERAL INFORMATION

Your restaurant's reputation will be built from the menu offering. In order to achieve the maximum yield for the money you are going to invest, each menu item must be considered in relation to the type of equipment you will need and the cost of that equipment. For example, hamburger: What is the amount of labor that is going to be needed to prepare, serve and clean up? What is the cost of utilities to operate that piece of equipment 10 to 14 hours a day? How much space and storage is needed? This must be weighed against buying hamburger patties already made.

By planning ahead you can avoid purchasing unneeded equipment. For instance, if you are going to use frozen, pre-fabricated meat cuts, ready sliced cheese, etc. this will determine the type of equipment you will need. If you are going to buy your potatoes already peeled there will be no need for a potato peeler.

It has often been said that a rule of thumb to follow in the allocation of space lay-out of a kitchen should represent 20–35 percent of the total usable area. But, if you use convenience foods this area could conceivably be less. An important factor to consider in the configuration of your kitchen is the shape. Is it square or is it rectangular? It makes a difference in terms of how the equipment is placed for maximum convenience and ease of operation, plus conformity to laws governing restaurants—health and fire codes, and other necessary requirements.

BASIC FACTS

1. Cater to the wants and needs in your area of service.
2. Start serving on time. If breakfast is to be served at 8:00 a.m. and your first customer arrives at 8:00 a.m. be prepared to serve whatever the order from the menu may be.
3. Keep records of the number of dishes sold daily.
4. Control leftovers.
5. Prepare items based on formula and cost (explained in another section in detail).
6. Have a good mix to offer on your menu.
7. The more you sell of an item, the lower your production cost will be.

MENU ANALYSIS

Once you have established the menu your customers will accept, you will know on both a weekly and monthly basis the items you will need to have available to prepare all the foods, as well as the dollar cost involved. You should then be able to predict your sales. By subtracting your operating cost you will have your net profit for that period with a fair degree of certainty.

SUMMARY: A successful restaurant's menu is no accident. It is a result of careful planning with many factors involved in making it a success. The experience of the owner in establishing proper formulas, updating costs, controlling leftovers, merchandising the menu and careful purchasing, are all important ingredients for a successful menu. A menu is more than a piece of paper listing food. Its objective should be to *sell* food.

Menus cycled anywhere from 2 weeks to 60 days or more in advance are well accepted by customers because each day something different appears.

Limited type service menus are outstanding in their acceptance by the food service industry.

In planning the menu try to balance the use of the equipment. For instance, don't run a menu on any one day which offers ten out of twelve items to be fried. This will over-tax your deep fryer and slow down service, which will irritate both customers and employees alike.

Make an easy-to-follow chart by listing all of the items on the menu in relation to the equipment needed.

EQUIPMENT	SOUP	SALAD	TURKEY	MEAT LOAF	JELLO	MILK	EGG SALAD	VEG.
Steam Table	X			X				
Refrigerator		X	X	X	X	X	X	
Slicer			X	X				
Pots	X							
Pans 12 x 20		X		X	X			
Chopper							X	
Can Opener								X
Ladle	X							

40

MENU IDEAS

Entrees

Eggs Benedict

Sauteed Snow Crab
Broiled Swordfish
Smelts
Broiled Trout
Broiled Scrod
Broiled Flounder
Broiled Halibut
Baked Crabmeat Casserole
Broiled Alaska King Crab Legs
Baked or Broiled Lobster
Baked Stuffed Lobster
Fried Oysters
Fried Fantail Shrimp
Fried Scallops
Fried Clams
Fried Filet of Sole
Fried Ipswich Clams
Shrimp Scampi
Fish & Chips with French Fries

Broiled Lamp Chops
Broiled Pork Chops
Broiled Beef Liver
   (with onions and/or bacon)
Broiled Calves Liver
   (with onions and/or bacon)
Broiled Sirloin Steak
Broiled chopped Sirloin
Filet Mignon
Roast Beef
Tenderloin of Beef
Chateau Briand
Meat Loaf
Mixed Grill of Filet
Beef Stew
Fried Chicken (half)
Boneless Breast of Chicken
Chicken Cacciatore
Chicken Pie
Chicken Cordon Bleu
Chicken Croquettes
Boiled Dinner
Corn Beef Hash
Spare Ribs
Duckling L'Orange
Baked Virginia Ham
Veal Francese
Veal Cordon Bleu

Note: It has been found that many customers will prefer
broiled fish and meat.

Hot Turkey Sandwich
Hot Roast Beef Sandwich

Pizza with
  Cheese
  Onion
  Peppers
  Anchovies
  Salami
  Mushrooms
  Pepperoni
  Linguica
  Italian Sausage
    (or any combination of above)

Veal Cutlet Parmesan
Spaghetti with Italian Sauce
Shell Macaroni
Baked Manicotti
Baked Lasagna
Eggplant Parmigiano

Soups

Clam Chowder (red or white)	Cabbage Soup
Onion Soup	Pea Soup
Chicken Broth	Chicken Noodle Soup
Beef Broth	Chicken Rice Soup
Bean Soup	Vegetable Soup
Mushroom Bisque	Vichyssoise
Tomato Bisque	Lobster Bisque
Borscht	

Juices

Orange	Prune
Grapefruit	Pineapple
Tomato	Mixed Vegetable
Cranberry	

Appetizers

Littlenecks on the half shell	Anchovies on Lettuce
Marinated Herring with Sour Cream	Blue Cheese Spread
Quiche Lorraine	Egg Rolls
Escargots Bourguignonne	Chicken Livers
Clams Casino	Oyster Stew
Marinated Mushrooms	Olives and Celery
Antipasto	Sardines
Freshly opened Oysters	Crackers and Cheese
Cherrystone Clams	Stuffed Quahaugs
Shrimp Cocktail	Fruit Cup

Salads

Caesar Salad	Julienne Salad
Chef Salad	Tunafish Salad
Antipasto	Chopped Chicken Livers
Tossed Green Salad	Egg Salad
Snail Salad	Shrimp Salad
Squid Salad	Pineapple and Cottage Cheese
Hearts of Lettuce	
Sliced Tomato and Lettuce	

Note: A salad bar would be another idea if you have the space. Any number of locally accepted items could be included.

Side Orders

French Fried Potatoes	Sauteed Onions
Fried Onion Rings	Cabbage
Lettuce and Tomato	Hard-boiled eggs
Cottage Cheese	Rice
Bacon	Asparagus
Sugar-cured Ham	Carrots
Cole Slaw	Sauerkraut
Mushrooms	Whipped Potatoes
Bagels	Lyonnaise Potatoes
Potato Salad	Delmonico Potatoes
Cherry Tomatoes	Home Fried Potatoes
Three Bean Salad	Baked Beans
Sliced Onions	Cranberry Sauce
Pickled Beets	Turkey Livers
Hot Vegetables	Clams
Baked Potato	Clam cakes
Macaroni Salad	
Cucumber Salad	

Sandwiches

Sardine	Egg Salad
Ham and Cheese	Western
Sliced Chicken	Peanut Butter and Jelly
Sliced Turkey	Liverwurst
Baked Ham	Pastromi
Salami	Steak
Sausage	Steak with Mushrooms
Meatball	Hamburger
Veal Cutlet	Cheeseburger
Sliced Tongue	Frankfurt
Chopped Liver	Frankfurt with Cheese
Hard-boiled egg	Crabmeat
Bacon, Lettuce and Tomato	Lobster Salad
Grilled Cheese	Barbequed Beef
Grilled Cheese with Bacon	Ham Salad
Grilled Cheese with Tomato	Reuben
Swiss Cheese	Salmon Salad
Fried Egg	Pepper Steak
Chicken Salad	Eggplant
Tuna Fish Salad	American Cheese
Shrimp Salad	Cream Cheese
Bologna	Cream Cheese and Olives

Combination Sandwiches (often called Club Sandwiches)
Ham, Tongue and Swiss Cheese
Turkey and chopped Liver
Hot Ham
Ham, Corned Beef and Swiss Cheese
Sardine, sliced Cheese and Hard-boiled Egg
Roast Beef and Swiss Cheese
Nova Scotia Lox, Cream Cheese and Onion
Lobster Salad

> Note: Combination or Club Sandwiches are usually toasted
> and made with three slices of bread.

Fruits

Grapefruit   (available when in season)
Orange and Grapefruit Sections
Baked Apple   Cantaloupe
Peach halves   Honeydew Melon
Sliced Bananas   Strawberries and Cream
Applesauce   Fresh Berries
Prunes

Desserts

Deep-dish Apple Pie   Chocolate Eclair
Chocolate Cream Pie   Cheese Tarts
Custard Pie   Cream Puffs
Lemon Meringue Pie   Baked Custard
Apple Pie   Tapioca Pudding
Apple Pie a la mode   Grapenut Pudding
Squash Pie   Chocolate Pudding
Blueberry Pie   Rice Pudding
Coconut Cream Pie   Raisin Cake
Strawberry Shortcake   Parfaits
N.Y. style Cheesecake   Ice Cream
Layer Cake   Spumoni with Claret Sauce
Jello   Banana Split
Coffee Gelatine   Sundaes

Beverages

Coffee   Milk
Tea   Hot Chocolate
Decaffeinated Coffee   Diet Beverages
Iced Coffee   Buttermilk
Iced Tea   Skimmed Milk

Breakfast

Eggs (cooked to order)	English Muffins
Omelet, plain	Bagel with Cream Cheese
Cheese Omelet	Cinnamon Toast
Ham and Cheese Omelet	Bacon Strips
Mushroom Omelet	Grilled Ham
French Toast	Sausages
Waffles	Canadian Bacon
Pancakes	Cold Cereals
Home Fries	Oatmeal

MENU: GENERAL INFORMATION—GARNISHES

Garnishes are used to decorate a dish with flavorsome and colorful trimmings that will add eye appeal to any meal. Following are some suggestions you may wish to use to generate more sales.

General

Slices/strips of pickle or small whole gherkin pickles
Thin slices or wedges of tomato
Pimiento strips
Sliced or whole radishes or radish roses
A wedge or slice of lemon
Shredded raw carrots, strips or curls
Crisp hearts of celery or celery curls
Strips or thin slices of cucumber
Strips or rings of green pepper
Pickled beets or onions
Watercress
Sprigs of fresh parsley
Mint leaves
A lettuce leaf
Slices or quarters of hard-boiled egg
Green or black olives, plain or stuffed
Cottage cheese, sweet relish or Chow-Chow in small souffle cup
Chopped or whole nuts
Whole or sliced maraschino cherries
Fresh berries in season

Garnishes for Hot Plates

Beef

Chili Sauce or Catsup
Any kind of pickle
Watercress or parsley

Chicken

Cranberry Sauce or Currant Jelly
Celery Stalks or Hearts
Olives, plain or stuffed
Sweet pickled peaches

Ham

A fruit glaze or sauce
Raisin sauce
Sauteed apple rings
Slices of pineapple or orange
Sweet and sour cole slaw or pineapple cole slaw

Hamburgers

Carrot strips or curls
Potato chips or french fried potatoes
Slice or spear of dill pickle
Small scoop of potato salad
Souffle cup of cole slaw

Pork

Apple sauce or spiced apple rings
Whole cranberry sauce, molded cranberry sauce or cranberry relish

Fish

A slice or wedge of lemon
A dusting of paprika
Celery and/or green pepper
Pickled onions or beets
Piccalilli or crisp pickle slices
Tartar sauce in lettuce cup or small souffle cup
Parsley or watercress
Cucumber slices, strips or relish
Spicy cole slaw
Green or black olives

PURCHASING FORM

Purpose

The objective of this form is to list every item that a restaurant needs in order to produce the menu. The menu needs are broken into categories (groceries, extracts, beverages, etc.) The form lists the ordered amount and the size. "OH" means what you presently have on hand. "O" means what you will be ordering. "T" means total.

This information if properly recorded each and every time, will give you important data for intelligent purchasing.

PURCHASING FORM					
Ord.	Size	Item	OH	O	T
		Grocery			
		Baking powder			
		Beans, wax			
		Beets, sliced			
		Belgian Carrots			
		Capers			
		Clam juice			
		Coffee–bean			
		Coffee–decaffeinated			
		Dry cereals			
		Dry milk powder			
		Gelatin, unflavored			
		Grapefruit juice, unsweetened			
		Hot cereals			
		Kitchen bouquet			
		Lemon juice			
		Lime juice			
		Mayonnaise, imitation			
		Mushrooms, P & S			
		Mushrooms, sliced			
		Mustard, hot			
		Mustard, prepared			
		Noodles, enriched			
		Orange juice			
		Pearl onions			
		Pimientos			
		Pineapple, chunks–natural juice			
		Pineapple, crushed–natural juice			
		Pineapple, sliced–natural juice			
		Pumpkin (canned)			
		Rice, enriched (Uncle Ben's)			
		Salmon, individual–3¾ oz.)			
		Salt			
		Sauerkraut			
		Skim Milk, evaporated			
		Soybean, dried			
		Spaghetti, enriched			
		Tabasco sauce			
		Tangerine juice			
		Tea			
		Tea, instant iced			
		Tomato juice			
		Tomato paste			
		Tomato puree			
		Tomato, whole			
		Tuna, individual–3¾ oz.			
		V-8 juice			
		Vinegar, cider			
		Worcestershire sauce			
		Yellow corn meal			
		Ziti			

PURCHASING FORM					
Ord.	Size	Item	OH	O	T
		Extracts			
		Brandy			
		Chocolate			
		Coconut			
		Maple			
		Lemon			
		Orange			
		Rum			
		Sherry			
		Vanilla			
		Beverages			
		Cherry			
		Chocolate			
		Cola			
		Cream			
		Ginger Ale			
		Lemon			
		Orange			
		Root Beer			
		Spices and Seasonings			
		Basil			
		Bay leaf			
		Celery salt			
		Chili powder			
		Cinnamon			
		Cloves, whole			
		Dill seed			
		Garlic powder			
		Nutmeg			
		Onion flakes—Dehydrated			
		Oregano			
		Paprika			
		Pepper, black			
		Pepper, white			
		Peppercorn			
		Poultry seasoning			
		Pumpkin pie spice			
		Rosemary			
		Tarragon			
		Thyme leaves			
		Fruit—Frozen			
		Berries			

PURCHASING FORM					
Ord.	Size	Item	OH	O	T
		Produce (Fresh)			
		Apples			
		Bananas			
		Blackberries			
		Blueberries			
		Cabbage			
		Cantaloupe			
		Carrots			
		Celery			
		Cucumbers			
		Eggplant			
		Garlic			
		Grapefruit, whole			
		Grapefruit sections (cold-pak)			
		Lemons			
		Lettuce			
		Limes			
		Melons, casaba			
		Melons, cranshaw			
		Melons, honeydew			
		Melons, Persian			
		Mint leaves			
		Onions, Bermuda			
		Onions, Spanish			
		Orange sections (cold-pak)			
		Parsley			
		Peaches			
		Peppers, Green			
		Pineapples			
		Potatoes			
		Radishes			
		Raspberries			
		Red cabbage			
		Strawberries			
		Tomatoes			
		Products (Frozen)			
		Broccoli			
		Cauliflower			
		Chicken breasts—8 oz. boneless			
		Chicken, diced			
		Green beans			
		Spinach			

PURCHASING FORM					
Ord.	Size	Item	OH	O	T
		Meats			
		Beef, cooked			
		Beef, diced			
		Beef, ground			
		Chicken, Cooked			
		Franks, all beef			
		Ham, Canned			
		Knockwurst, all beef			
		Liver, calves			
		Livers, chicken			
		Pork, diced			
		Skirt steak			
		Strip loin (8 or 10 oz.)			
		Top round			
		Turkey, cooked (natural-shape breasts)			
		Veal, ground			
		Veal steaks			
		Seafood			
		Crab meat			
		Langostino			
		Lobster meat			
		Salmon, smoked			
		Scallops			
		Shrimp, PDQ (16–20)			
		Sole, filet			
		Dairy			
		Buttermilk			
		Cheese, American			
		Cheese, cottage			
		Cheese, Swiss			
		Eggs			
		Margarine, diet			
		Margarine, pats (1 teaspoon per)			
		Skim milk			
		Bake			
		Rolls, 1 oz.			
		Enriched white bread			
		Whole wheat bread			
		Miscellaneous			
		Beef broth			
		Blue cheese salad dressing			
		Chicken broth–Seasoning Mix			
		French salad dressing mix			
		Italian Dressing Mix			
		Italian dry sauce mix			
		Orange			
		Root beer			

PURCHASING FORM					
Ord.	Size	Item	OH	O	T
		Take-out—Paper Items			
	8 oz. cold	Juice			
		Fruits			
	10 oz. w/lid	Coffee, hot			
	16 oz. cold w/lid	Iced coffee			
	10 oz. hot	Hot tea			
	16 oz. cold	Iced tea			
	10 oz. hot	Hot chocolate			
	24 oz. cold	Chocolate milk			
	10 oz. cold	Skim milk			
	10 oz. cold	Buttermilk			
	16 oz. cold	Milkshake			
		Salad plate w/dome—9"			
		#4 Bag, flat			
		#6 Bag, flat			
		#20 Bag, flat			
		clear salad, 8 oz.			
		clear salad, 6 oz.			
		Guest checks			
		Straws, large			
		Forks, knives, spoons, plastic			
		Wax paper, jumbo			
		4 x 4 portion paper			
		Meat covering paper			
		Hot pack containers			
		Soup containers			
		Sundae dish, 5 oz. w/lid			
		Spoons			
		Coffee stirrers			
		Napkins			
		7" alum, plate			
		9" plate w/dome—hot foods			
		18" roll wrap			

OPEN ORDER SHEET—KITCHEN NEEDS

This form can be used very effectively to determine the needs in each area of your restaurant. Go through the menu, visualize what is needed to make up every item, then put it in the section where needed. For example, if you come to brown gravy you know you will need a ladle. This would be placed in the kitchen area. You will also need pans, with covers, in this area. List the amounts and describe the items so that when you go to purchase them you will have a prepared list as a reference.

OPEN ORDER SHEET

Qty.	Unit	Description
	Ea.	Flour sifters
	Ea.	Nonstick muffin pans
	Ea.	Cake testers
	Ea.	Lemon boards
	Ea.	Fruit knives
	Ea.	Grapefruit knives
	Ea.	Measuring cups
	Ea.	Parers and corers
	Ea.	1/2-size hotel pans
	Ea.	S/S measuring spoons
	Ea.	2 oz. ladles
	Ea.	Egg poachers
	Ea.	Nonstick omelet pans
	Ea.	1 qt. dry measures
	Ea.	1 gallon measures
	Ea.	3 oz. ladles
	Ea.	1/9-size pans w/covers
	Ea.	H.B. single mixers
	Ea.	Tongs—plastic
	Ea.	#5 can openers
	Ea.	Slotted spoons
	Ea.	Salad spreaders
	Ea.	Hamburg offset
	Ea.	4 oz. ladles
	Ea.	6 oz. ladles
	Ea.	5 1/2 qt. heavy bottom sauce pans w/covers
	Ea.	7 1/2 qt. heavy bottom sauce pans w/covers
	Ea.	9″ x 9″ nonstick baking pans
	Ea.	Cake lifters
	Ea.	8 oz. ladles
	Ea.	13 qt. mixing bowls
	Ea.	Spaghetti strainers
	Ea.	Spray bottles
	Ea.	Lacy hot cup
	Ea.	Meat grinder
	Ea.	Lettuce machine
	Ea.	Waring Blender gallon size, s/s and quart size
	Ea.	Broiler racks
	Ea.	S/S dish to house 3 ea. #12 scoops
	Ea.	#5 Jr. Edlund
	Ea.	Dredges
	Ea.	Cheese graters

OPEN ORDER SHEET

Qty.	Unit	Description
	Ea.	1/2-size sheet pans
	Ea.	Portion scales
	Ea.	2 wheel trucks
	Ea.	Full-size hotel pans—2 1/2″ deep w/covers
	Ea.	1/2-size hotel pans—2 1/2″ deep w/covers
	Ea.	1/4-size hotel pans—2 1/2″ deep w/covers
	Ea.	1/6-size hotel pans—2 1/2″ deep w/covers
	Ea.	Full-size hotel pans—4″ deep w/covers
	Ea.	1/2-size hotel pans—4″ deep w/covers
	Ea.	1/4-size hotel pans—4″ deep w/covers
	Ea.	1/6-size hotel pans—4″ deep w/covers
	Ea.	Full-size hotel pans—6″ deep w/covers
	Ea.	1/2 size hotel pans—6″ deep w/covers
	Ea.	1/4-size hotel pans—6″ deep w/covers
	Ea.	1/6-size hotel pans—6″ deep w/covers
	Ea.	Bristol floor matting—all small
	Ea.	Can opener
	Ea.	Plate covers
	Ea.	Spatulas
	Ea.	First-aid kits
	Ea.	Solid spoons s/s (basting)
	Ea.	Slotted spoons s/s
	Ea.	Deck brush w/handle
	Ea.	Bench brush
	Ea.	S.H. pot brush (nylon)
	Ea.	Sponges—large
	Boxes	Chore Boy towels
	Ea.	Oven trays 18″ x 26″ x 1″
	Ea.	Funnels, s/s
	Ea.	Push carts, 3 shelves
	Pair	Rubber gloves
	Ea.	Paddle
	Ea.	Tomato King slicer
	Ea.	Double boilers
	Ea.	Peelers—celery
	Ea.	Pan handlers
	Ea.	Oven brush
	Ea.	Double mesh strainers
	Ea.	Single mesh strainers
	Ea.	Pencil sharpeners
	Ea.	Pot forks
	Ea.	China cap—fine—small w/pot
	Ea.	Soap dispensers w/soap

OPEN ORDER SHEET

Qty.	Unit	Description
	Ea.	Squeegee
	Ea.	Towel holders
	Ea.	Mop and wringer
	Ea.	Brooms
	Ea.	Small ingredient bins
	Ea.	File cabinet
	Ea.	Pie markers 4 1/2″
	Ea.	Roast pans
	Ea.	Scissors
	Ea.	Sugar bowl filler
	Ea.	Egg beaters
	Ea.	Dust pans—bench brushes
	Ea.	Ice scoops
	Ea.	Box openers
	Ea.	Skimmers
	Ea.	Flour bins
	Ea.	Mincers
	Ea.	Knife rack holders
	Doz.	Decanters for salt
	Ea.	Icing grates 12″ x 18″
	Ea.	Custard cups, individual
	Ea.	Dressing servers for: French, Italian, Blue Cheese, Russian
	Ea.	Piano whips—8″
	Ea.	Piano whips—12″
	Ea.	Piano whips—18″
	Ea.	Spatulas—8″
	Ea.	Spatulas—10″
	Ea.	Spatulas—12″
	Ea.	Hamburger breather cover
	Ea.	French whip—12″
	Ea.	French whip—18″
	Ea.	Spring tongs—6″
	Ea.	Spring tongs—12″
	Ea.	Spring tongs—18″
	Ea.	Oven thermometers
	Ea.	Refrigerator thermometers
	Ea.	Freezer thermometers
	Ea.	Pastry brushes—1″
	Ea.	Pastry brushes—2″
	Ea.	Pastry brushes—3″
	Ea.	Torpedo waste receptacles
	Ea.	12 qt. alum. stock pots w/covers
	Ea.	24 qt. alum. stock pots w/covers

OPEN ORDER SHEET

Qty.	Unit	Description
	Ea.	16 qt. alum. stock pots w/covers
	Ea.	40 qt. alum. stock pots w/covers
	Ea.	#8 H.B. scoops
	Ea.	#12 H.B. scoops
	Ea.	#16 H.B. scoops
	Ea.	#20 H.B. scoops
	Ea.	#24 H.B. scoops
	Ea.	Push brooms—18″
	Ea.	Push brooms—24″
	Ea.	Alum. fry pans—8″
	Ea.	Alum. fry pans—10″
	Ea.	Alum. fry pans—12″
	Ea.	Alum. fry pans—14″
	Ea.	1 1/2 qt. alum. sauce pans w/covers
	Ea.	2 1/2 qt. alum. sauce pans w/covers
	Ea.	3 1/2 qt. alum. sauce pans w/covers
	Ea.	4 1/2 qt. alum. sauce pans w/covers
	Ea.	5 1/2 qt. alum. sauce pans w/covers
	Ea.	78710 Bainmarie w/covers
	Ea.	78720 Bainmarie w/covers
	Ea.	78730 Bainmarie w/covers
	Ea.	78740 Bainmarie w/covers
	Ea.	78760 Bainmarie w/covers
	Ea.	78780 Bainmarie w/covers
	Ea.	78820 Bainmarie w/covers
	Ea.	78154 Vegetable inset w/covers
	Ea.	78164 Vegetable inset w/covers
	Ea.	78184 Vegetable inset w/covers
	Ea.	78204 Vegetable inset w/covers
	Ea.	68750 s/s mixing bowls
	Ea.	69014 s/s mixing bowls
	Ea.	69030 s/s mixing bowls
	Ea.	69040 s/s mixing bowls
	Ea.	69050 s/s mixing bowls
	Ea.	69080 s/s mixing bowls
	Ea.	Plastic storage containers—8 qt. w/covers
	Ea.	Plastic storage containers—12 qt. w/covers
	Ea.	Plastic storage containers—16 qt. w/covers

Sandwich Grill Area

Qty.	Unit	Description
	Ea.	Steak weights
	Ea.	Sandwich weights
	Ea.	Alum. trays—10″ x 12″

OPEN ORDER SHEET

Qty.	Unit	Description
	Ea.	Rubber spatulas
	Ea.	Knife sharpener
	Ea.	Check holders, infra-holder
	Ea.	Broiler brush
	Ea.	1/2 size hotel pans 2 1/2" deep w/covers
	Ea.	1/3 size hotel pans 2 1/2" deep w/covers
	Ea.	1/4 size hotel pans 2 1/2" deep w/covers
	Ea.	1/6 size hotel pans 2 1/2" deep w/covers
	Ea.	1/9 size hotel pans 2 1/2" deep w/covers
	Ea.	1/2 size hotel pans 4" deep w/covers
	Ea.	1/3 size hotel pans 4" deep w/covers
	Ea.	1/4 size hotel pans 4" deep w/covers
	Ea.	1/6 size hotel pans 4" deep w/covers
	Ea.	1/9 size hotel pans 4" deep w/covers
	Ea.	1/4 paring knife
	Ea.	Cleaver
	Ea.	Boner
	Ea.	Cook's knife—10"
	Ea.	Cook's knife—12"
	Ea.	Slicer
	Ea.	Steel (sharpening)
	Ea.	Bread knife
	Ea.	Utility knife
	Ea.	Sandwich spreader
	Ea.	Steak knife
Refrigerator Needs		
	Ea.	Plungers
Take-Out Section		
	Ea.	Spindles for checks
Top of Table		
	Doz.	Steak knives
	Doz.	Teaspoons—Linford
	Doz.	Knives
	Doz.	Forks—Linford
	Doz.	Bouillon spoons—Linford
	Doz.	Dessert spoons—Linford
	Doz.	Iced teaspoons—Linford
	Doz.	Oyster forks—Linford
	Ea.	Cake stands
	Ea.	Cake covers
	Ea.	Clipboards

OPEN ORDER SHEET

Qty.	Unit	Description
	Ea.	Ashtrays s/s
	Ea.	Cash boxes
	Ea.	Bus boxes 15" x 20"
	Ea.	Silver bins
	Ea.	Bus boxes, 1/2 size
	Ea.	Milk pitchers—1/2 size capacity—white or s/s
	Ea.	Oyster cups
	Ea.	Mustard spoons
	Ea.	Cheese shakers
	Ea.	Decanters to store flour, 1 lb. capacity
	Ea.	Napkin dispensers
	Ea.	3-way server—Vollrath w/covers
	Ea.	Reserved signs
	Ea.	Insulated coffee servers 32–64 oz.
	Ea.	Pepper mills
	Ea.	Vinegar cruets
	Ea.	Water pitchers, 64 oz.
	Ea.	Teapots, 10 oz.
	Ea.	Candle holders
	Ea.	Ingredient bins

Dish Room Needs

	Ea.	Barrels—32 gal. w/covers
	Ea.	Silver bins
	Ea.	Racks for dishes
	Ea.	Racks for glasses
	Ea.	Silver racks
	Ea.	Carrying rack

Liquor Section

	Ea.	S/S pails for ice—13 qt.
	Ea.	Plastic ice scoops
	Roll	Aero liner

Cleaning Supplies
& Paper Products

	Case	Chin wipers
	Case	Floor compound
	Case	Sip stix
	Case	S/S polish
	Case	Alum. foil wrap
	Case	Alum. souffle cups—1/2 oz.
	Case	Alum. souffle cups—1 oz.

OPEN ORDER SHEET

Qty.	Unit	Description
Rest Rooms		
	Case	Soap
	Case	Women's needs
	Ea.	Bowl brushes
Receiving—Storage Area		
	Ea.	Toolbox complete
	Ea.	Receiving scale
	Ea.	Skids—wood
	Ea.	2-wheel trucks
	Ea.	Plumber's snake
	Ea.	4-wheel truck
Front of House		
	Ea.	Baby chairs—high chairs
	Ea.	Clocks
	Ea.	Gaychrome stands
	Ea.	Lobby pans & brushes
	Ea.	Sand urns—wood grain
	Ea.	Registers
	Ea.	Coat hangers—racks
	Ea.	Champagne stand—complete brush gold
	Ea.	Stapler and staples
	Ea.	Pencils
	Ea.	Writing pads
	Ea.	Vacuum cleaner
Parking Lot		
	Ea.	Garage broom
	Ea.	25 ft. hose
	Ea.	Shovels
	Ea.	Ice breaker
	Ea.	Lawn rake

MEALS SOLD DAILY

The attached form will prove a valuable tool when used to count the number of meals sold daily. It will be an excellent referral source the next time the same items are put on the menu.

This kind of information compiled over a given period will help you to plan so there will not be a large amount of food left over, nor will you run short.

MEALS SOLD DAILY

Number Sold   Date Week Ending _____

Item	Price	Sun.	Mon.	Tues.	Wed.	Thur.	Fri.	Sat.	Total Sold	Total $

GENERAL MENU INFORMATION

The suggested size for a clip-on to your menu to run specials is 3"
x 4 1/2".

Helpful hints for setting up your menu.

GOOD MORNING! WE'VE BEEN EXPECTING YOU

It's a pleasure to welcome you as a first time visitor and a double
pleasure to welcome you as a regular guest!

NO. 1
Juice
TWO EGGS
Home Fries, Toast, Coffee

NO. 2
Juice
TWO GRIDDLE CAKES
Butter and syrup
Coffee or Tea

NO. 3
Juice
GOLDEN BROWN FRENCH TOAST
Butter, syrup or jelly
Coffee

NO. 4
Juice
TWO EGGS
Bacon or Sausage
Home Fries, Toast, Coffee

NO. 5
Juice
HAM AND EGGS
Home Fries, Toast, Coffee

NO. 6
Juice
BREAKFAST STEAK
Two country fresh eggs
Hot buttered toast
Coffee

JUICES
Tomato Juice
Orange Juice
Grapefruit Juice
Pineapple Juice

CEREALS
COLD CEREAL
with milk
with Half & Half
HOT CEREAL
with milk
with Half and Half

BEVERAGES
Hot coffee
Hot tea
Hot chocolate
Fresh milk
Sanka

FRUITS
Sliced peaches
1/2 cantalope (in season)
1/2 grapefruit (in season)
Fruit cocktail

More helpful hints for setting up your menu.

WELCOME! IT'S BREAKFAST TIME

EGGS AND OMELETTES

HAM AND EGGS—Potatoes, Toast, Butter or Jelly
BACON AND EGGS—Potatoes, Toast, Butter or Jelly
SAUSAGE AND EGGS—Potatoes, Toast, Butter or Jelly
TWO EGGS—Potatoes, Toast, Butter or Jelly
PLAIN OMELETTE—Potatoes, Toast, Butter or Jelly
CHOPPED HAM OMELETTE—Potatoes, Toast, Butter or Jelly
CHEESE OMELETTE—Potatoes, Toast, Butter or Jelly
TWO POACHED EGGS on Buttered Toast, Potatoes
TWO EGGS—any style, with Home-Baked Beans, Toast, Butter or Jelly,
          Potatoes, Coffee
ONE EGG—Home Fries, Toast, Butter or Jelly, Coffee
ONE EGG—with Ham, Bacon or Sausage

CORNED BEEF HASH AND ONE EGG—Toast

Hot Cakes

HOT CAKES (3)—Syrup and Butter
HOT CAKES AND BACON—Syrup and Butter
HOT CAKES AND HAM—Syrup and Butter
BLUEBERRY HOT CAKES, Syrup and Butter, Coffee

Sandwiches

Ham Sandwich   American Cheese
Ham and Egg   Grilled Cheese
Bacon and Egg   Cheese Eastern
Fried Egg

Side Orders

HOMEMADE MUFFINS—Bran, Corn, Blueberry w/Butter
HOME BAKED BEANS with Toast
SIDE OF FRENCH FRIES
              GRILLED HAM
              PORK SAUSAGE
              BACON STRIPS
              BREAKFAST ROLL
              GOLDEN TOAST
              DANISH PASTRY
              ENGLISH MUFFIN w/Jelly

The following is a suggested form to use as a daily changeable flyer:

DATE ___

BILL'S RESTAURANT

Luncheon Specials Served Daily
11:00 a.m. to 4:30 p.m. except Sundays

BILL'S SPECIAL
List your special here

TODAY'S ENTREES

1. -

2. -

3. -

4. -

5. -

6. -

7. -

8. -

*   Rolls & Butter served w/Dinners
(Other than Sandwiches)

SOUP AND SANDWICH SPECIAL

Here list the special

BEVERAGES

1. - Coffee, Tea

2. -

3. -

DESSERTS

1. - Pie

2. - Cake

3. - Strawberry Shortcake

The following are some helpful suggestions to consider when making your menu headings, i.e. appetizers, soups, salads, etc.:

APPETIZER

Note—If possible list appetizers that are popular and will hold up if you don't sell a large amount. Also remember the appetizer that doesn't sell today will have lost its freshness the next day.

SOUPS

Note—Always list whether it is available in cup or bowl, or both— include crackers, roll, bread w/butter on the menu. Be sure you figure these last-mentioned items in your cost.

SALADS

Note—For excellent customer acceptance be sure your waiters/ waitresses suggest appetizers and salads to all patrons. If you sell many salads they should be made up in advance and put in the open-view refrigerated display case to encourage impulse buying.

DINNERS

Note—Be sure the customer can easily tell from the menu if he/she gets a roll, salad, bread w/butter. Spell it out clearly.

SEAFOOD DINNERS

Note—Mix price structuring of menu items. For example, do not list all $7.00 dinners on one side. Mix and match dishes as they relate to prices.

CHILDREN'S OR SENIOR CITIZEN'S ORDERS, AND SPECIAL DIETS

Note—Be sure to consider both of these. Also consider people on special diets, for example low cholesterol, those who can't have salt in their food, etc. Customers are sure to appreciate your thoughtfulness.

DESSERTS

Note—This item can also be cut, plated and placed in open-view display cases for impulse buying.

BEVERAGES

*Note—*The old standbys are coffee, tea and hot chocolate. However, continental coffees and a decaffeinated coffee are also good items to feature.

Note: Make up a card or sheet for every item you serve. This will insure that everyone makes it the same way every time as your cost is figured on each plate.

Remember that as cost goes up you must adjust your selling price. The following information is the type of explanation you should use for each item on the menu.

GRILLED EGGS WITH BACON (ONE SERVING)

2 eggs
2 slices bacon (buy hotel pack—you get more strips that way)
2 oz. french fried potatoes
2 slices of toast
2 pats of butter (120 count)
1 cup of coffee

Method of Preparation

1. Heat griddle to 350°
2. Grease with oleo
3. When eggs, bacon and potatoes are cooked place on 9" plate.
4. Place eggs in middle, bacon on one side and potatoes on the other
5. Serve toast with butter (no jelly unless requested)

Suggestions

Dry bacon well
Serve any time of day

COST BREAKDOWN

Potato, bread and coffee	.30¢
Eggs	.25
Total cost	.55¢
10% shrinkage factor	.60
Selling price	$1.75
Gross profit	65%

MENUS FOR SPECIAL OCCASIONS

On special occasions such as Father's Day, Mother's Day, Christmas, etc. it becomes imperative that you place more plates, cups, saucers and flatware into use in your restaurant to make sure that when you are busy all items will be available.

Sometimes in a busy restaurant the usual daily menu is not offered. A special one-day menu is usually printed on inexpensive place mats, paper sheets, etc. This is done to scale down the number of menu items offered to speed up service, keep customers satisfied and turn over the seats more quickly to serve the maximum number of people.

HAPPY FATHER'S DAY

APPETIZERS

Oysters Casino

Tomato Juice

Fresh Fruit w/Sherbet

Celery

Olives, Green or Black

Jumbo Shrimp Cocktail—Sm. Lg.

Atlantic Blue Crab Cocktail
  (when available)

Imported Sardines with Lettuce and Onion

Provolone Cheese & Crackers (small)

Crackers w/Cheese

Clams Oregnato (6)

SOUPS (cups)

Oyster Stew

Chicken Soup

ITALIAN STYLE SALADS

Small

Medium

Large

BLACK ANGUS SPECIAL

Shrimp Cocktail

Soup—Potato—Vegetable—Salad

BLACK ANGUS (SIRLOIN) 1 1/2 lb.

Strawberry Shortcake

Roll and Butter—Coffee

TENDERLOIN EN BROCHETTE

Beef broiled on a skewer with Peppers,
Onions and Mushrooms
Served with Rice and Vegetable

Roast Boneless Stuffed Chicken
  w/Mushroom Cap

Broiled Hawaiian Ham Steak

OUR FAMOUS OPEN STEAK

(Tenderloin)

FILET MIGNON

ITALIAN DINNERS

Italian style Veal Cutlets

Italian style Veal Parmesan

CHOPS

Broiled Pork Chops

Broiled Lamb Chops

French Fries, Mashed or Baked Potatoes,
Hot Buttered Carrots, String Beans,
Cole Slaw or Beets

All Dinners a La Carte

Potato, Spaghetti or Macaroni and Vegetable included with
above dinners

Peppers in place of Potato or Vegetable—Extra

Order of Fried Peppers

Side order of Mushrooms

LOBSTER
Fresh Lobster Saute en Casserole
(w/toast points)
Lobster Salad

SHRIMP
Baked Stuffed Shrimp, Drawn Butter
Shrimp Salad Plate

SHELLFISH
Native Scallops
Snow Crab Saute, Toast Points

FISH
Baked Scrod w/Lobster Dressing
Sword Fish (when available)

CHILDREN'S ORDERS (12 and under)
and
SENIOR CITIZEN'S ORDERS
Veal Cutlets
Spaghetti or Macaroni
Scallops
Pork Chop
Lamb Chop
Open Steak
Hot Turkey (all white meat)
Hot Turkey (white & dark meat)
Hamburg Plate
Spaghetti and Sausage
Circus Cocktail

DESSERTS
Pie (fresh baked)
Pie a la Mode
Ice Cream
Chocolate Fudge Sundae
Strawberry Shortcake
Strawberry Sundae
Grasshopper Pie
Cherry Cheese Cake
Tortoni

Creme de Menthe Parfait
Spumoni (Claret)
Pie and Cheese
Jello
Pudding
Strawberry Parfait
Hot Fudge Parfait
Pecan Pie
Galliano Parfait
Spumoni Eclair

BEVERAGES
Tea
Coffee
Iced Coffee
Espresso (cup)
Decaffeinated Coffee
Iced Tea
Soda
Milk
Low-fat Milk
Diet Soda

COFFEES OF THE WORLD
Jewish
French
Greek
Irish
Italian
Jamaican
The Magnificent Cappuccino
(mug extra)

In order to serve you better we have limited our menu for
FATHER'S DAY

QUESTIONS

1. The menu is the blueprint of the restaurant.

   True ___   False ___

2. What is a menu flier?

3. What is a menu rider?

4. Featuring foods that are plentiful and/or economical makes sense.

   True ___   False ___

5. Menus should be left where customers can easily pick them up.

   True ___   False ___

6. What is the purpose of a menu?

7. What is a formula preparation?

8. List five things that would increase sales and tips.

7
Purchasing, Storage, Receiving, Planning

Good purchasing practices result in getting the right product at the time you want it, and getting it delivered to the right place and at the price you agreed to pay. You must learn the market as it relates to the purchase of food, equipment and supplies with their variable quality, price and availability. You can buy with confidence and buy competitively once you get to know the market. One way to accomplish this is to take courses in purchasing and related food services, and management techniques prior to opening your business. Once you do open, you should always strive to learn more.

You must learn specified purchasing by *weight, grade, hold-up ability of product, quality* and year-round standards you establish for yourself in purchasing. For example, you may want a specific brand of tuna at a specific weight. You can compare price, delivery and quality in order to set up the standards that will best fit your menu needs. In this way, you can fix your cost of operation.

CONTRACT VOLUME PURCHASING

When a certain item on your menu is being sold in such volume that you are ordering in very large quantities you may want to contract with your supplier for a set amount (based on your knowledge of how the item sells) for a given period of time, at a given price. The danger in this method is that if the market drops in price you could be locked in at the higher price.

SPECIFIC PURCHASING

It is usually safest to buy your daily needs, and pay on a monthly basis. When you decide what supplies are to be delivered, check the following items and make sure they are understood by your supplier:

1. Brand name desired.
2. Grade, weight or count of item.
3. Size of container.
4. Quality.
5. Year-round availability.
6. Delivery time and place.
7. Back-ordered items. Will you allow your supplier to substitute?
8. Emergency deliveries.
9. Hours your suppliers are open.
10. Policy on damaged goods.
11. Consistent quality of items that are made especially for you. For example, if you and your supplier of hamburger agree on a set amount of shrinkage after cooking (Let us say that a 4 oz. hamburger will shrink to 3 1/2 oz.), check it occasionally, say once every month or so, to be certain you are getting the formula you are paying for. The formula is based on the amount of fat mixed into the meat. The fat content varies depending on the quality of hamburger. You will find out by regular checking whether your supplier is "on the level," or whether lower-quality hamburger is being substituted.

RECEIVING

The following are guidelines to follow in receiving, which is a vital part of operating a restaurant.

1. Before you sign any bill, check it thoroughly to make sure you have got what you ordered.

2. List all items received. Use an incoming delivery report. This will enable you to compare items such as price and packaging over any period of time.

3. You will need dollies or a castered platform rack to move heavy items. This expense will eventually pay for itself by saving goods from damage.

4. If you are unable to receive the goods yourself give the job to a reliable person, but you should spot-check receiving as often as possible.

5. Have a specific area where all supplies and goods are received. Be sure it's big enough. An efficient method of checking and distribution to other parts of the restaurant is essential.

6. Be sure that the person designated to do the checking knows all your purchasing specifications.

7. Weigh all items bought by weight, and count all items bought singly or by the case.

8. Stamp the date received and price paid on all items, containers, cases, boxes, etc. This will enable you to compare prices, and will help spot price increases when you reorder. Putting the price on the item also makes employees realize that the product they are handling does cost money!

9. Refrigerate items that need refrigeration *immediately.*

10. Put everything in a locked place immediately upon delivery. Items left out frequently disappear.

11. Keep the receiving door locked at all times. Keep strangers out of the stock area.

12. Allow no employee to sign for deliveries other than the person assigned to this responsibility.

13. Keep related items (such as paper cups and lids) next to each other.

14. When you store cases, tear off the top of the carton for easy access to the item. You may need it in a hurry.

STORAGE

All employees must be trained in the proper way to store foods.

1. Place cases on skids rather than directly on floor.
2. Store items used most often within easy reach, close to the place where they will be used.
3. Rotate the stock. What comes in first should be used first.

4. Keep food away from walls.
5. Foods that will create odors in a refrigerator should be stored separately.
6. Keep cleaning items separated from food items.
7. *Do not use* swollen cans of vegetables, fruits, etc. If credit cannot be received for them, discard at once.

It is the owner/operator's responsibility to check the following:

1. Proper ventilation in the storeroom.
2. Engage a pest control company to treat the entire restaurant on a regular basis.
3. Refrigerators and freezers must be checked regularly by a competent refrigeration company.
4. Thermometers should be kept in refrigerators, freezers and stock room. Temperatures should be checked often.
5. Take a physical inventory once a month at least.

RELATED INFORMATION

1. All employees should enter and leave from the front door.
2. Packages received should be inspected by you and need to be inventoried by you.
3. Keep control of all keys and, if possible, put a time-lock on the front door so you know when the door is opened and locked, and by whom.
4. Separate your food expense from cleaning supplies, repairs, etc. in your accounting. The benefits of doing this will be explained, in detail, by your accountant. This method will help you determine the true cost of the food.
5. Keep your suppliers to a minimum but never get locked in with one supplier. Have an alternate you can go to in case of a problem with your major supplier.

PERPETUAL INVENTORY CONTROL SHEET (see sample on page 73)

1. This control form should be located on a clipboard in your storeroom. Under the initial heading marked "ITEM" inventory

Perpetual Inventory Control Sheet

Item	Col. 1	Col. 2	Col. 3	Col. 4	Col. 5

everything in your locked storeroom. In column 1—write the number of items you have in stock. In column 2—when an item is taken, the amount taken must be subtracted. Then when a new delivery is made, this must be added in column 3. This process is continued on and on. At any time you can look at this clipboard and know just how much of anything you have on hand. This discourages stealing, and employees quickly learn whether you are truly keeping an eagle eye on supplies.

2.   Remember that a clean, neat and locked storeroom will pay big dividends to you in profits.

3.   Employees' cars should not be allowed to be parked near the back door of the kitchen. This rule makes it difficult, or impossible for a dishonest employee to put food in his/her car at your expense.

PLANNING AND GENERAL INFORMATION

A good aspect of the food service industry is that you have a fast turnover of the product. In most other businesses inventory can lie dormant for years. A new owner/operator should start buying in small quantities until he/she establishes a usage factor through keeping accurate records. Remember, you can always re-order at any time.

If you can get a supplier close to your place of business you will be able to have more frequent deliveries, which may be an important factor to consider. If your supplier is farther away, deliveries may be made only every two weeks. You must consider this in your planning. It may also be possible for you to pick up deliveries yourself.

Bread, pastry and milk orders must be made daily. A controlled, perpetual inventory sheet is the most important thing you can use to help you in your purchasing.

Sales checks can play an important part in helping you plan for purchasing. You must study the checks to see what has been sold and cross check your stock to see if they agree. This also helps you establish a trend that will tell you what to prepare for week after week. Leftovers become costly and unprofitable to you. Small items and factors, as well as large ones must be watched closely. Proper planning and forecasting is the key to making a profit.

ORDERING FOR THE MENU

The menu is the first thing you must plan. Once this is established you can make a list of all the items you will need. The following list will help you with the food portion of it:

Major Item Entree	Inventory Needed to Produce Major Item Entree
Beef Stew	Potatoes, carrots, onions, beef, celery, salt, pepper
Baked Tuna Noodle	Tuna, noodles, oleo, cheese, milk, flour, salt, pepper
Chili	Ground beef, peppers, onions, salt, chili powder, paprika, dry red beans, tomatoes
Manhattan Clam Chowder	Clams, tomatoes, carrots, peppers, onions, celery, potatoes, salt, pepper

GENERAL INFORMATION

Make a master file of every delivery company you buy from and include name, address, city, state, telephone number. Keep it handy where you can quickly refer to it.

Try to eliminate paying C.O.D. for deliveries. It is not wise to allow a storeroom clerk to get involved in paying for C.O.D.'s. If you must pay in this fashion, *always* handle the transaction yourself.

ORDERING

A salesperson's first responsibility is to sell his/her product to you. Most of them are well trained and can be helpful in making suggestions—they pick up many ideas going from restaurant to restaurant. They can also inform you of new trends in the industry, upcoming trade shows you can visit which will show you what is happening on a nation, or area wide basis, and what magazines and pamphlets to subscribe to. This will help you to extend the never-ending learning process.

BILLING

Discuss your method of billing with your suppliers from the beginning. Some companies want daily payments, whereas others bill monthly. If you develop a good paying record, companies will always look at you with favor when it comes to good prices, specials and emergency deliveries. A good supplier can be relied upon during strikes, bad weather, etc. You must constantly check all deliveries and let suppliers know you are checking. Another important point: File all delivery copies immediately, first checking for amounts, items ordered, price, etc.

PORTION CONTROL

Portion control is the ability to buy fish, hamburger, poultry and many other items in a specific size, mostly ready to use. This eliminates the need for specialized kitchen help. In most cases the cost of the portion control item is often reflected in the cost which the restaurant operator must pass on to the customer. The big advantage of portion control items is their exact size, controlled quality and speed of preparation, all of which are so vital to every owner/operator.

GENERAL INFORMATION

It is a good idea to track your food inventory stock. You may buy a 5 lb. box of a product and then find that it will last you for 3 years. Try buying a smaller size and you can eliminate the dead items you will accumulate through trying new items that do not sell. You will find the box still in inventory if you don't track the item based on how it is consumed in your business. Try to return the unopened cans or boxes to the supplier. In this manner you will not tie up dollars you need to keep successful. If you are unable to return these items for full credit, run specials and use them up. Whatever you do don't let such items "sit," they lose money for you that way.

Don't overstock inventory. If a person knows there are 15 or 20 steaks on hand and one or two get overcooked he/she will not be too concerned knowing there are more to fall back on. If there are only a few to work with, the person in question will naturally be more careful. Low inventory eliminates waste, gives you more room, better rotation of stock, and doesn't tie up dollars.

PLANNING AND FORECASTING

Planning can also be done from the sales checks. For example; if 15 orders of ham were cut in the morning and when the checks are analyzed only 11 were sold, you then should see if 4 are left over. Keeping records of meals sold will establish a trend that will tell you what to prepare week after week. You must closely watch the actual time you run out of a specific item. You may get different trends in food acceptance each time. You don't want to run out too early. Leftovers are costly and unprofitable so attention to usage factors over a period of time will show you what to prepare.

SUMMARY: Purchasing is directly related to your menu and performs the following:

1. Purchasing buys all your menu items and all other supplies necessary to do business.
2. How much you pay for any item is an important factor in establishing the selling price to the customer.
3. Your expertise in the purchase of food, equipment and other related items will determine the quality of the food served, the surroundings and the ultimate success of the business.

Purchasing is a vital factor for the success of a business. It must be given proper time and attention and the rewards will be profitable.

COOKING SUGGESTIONS

The cook or chef normally takes responsibility for preparing meals but what if he/she should be sick or on vacation? Are recipes available to the person taking over as cook? Do instructions include all the little "extras" that make the food special? Do recipes explain how to make a good gravy; what to do to canned vegetables to make them more acceptable; what to do to make meats tender and flavorful, etc.? As an example, hamburgers, the favorite of most Americans, should be juicy to insure customer's satisfaction.

This can be achieved by using the best grade of beef and cooking it slowly at the correct temperature. There is nothing worse than ordering a hamburger and getting a thin, dried out patty. This same procedure should be used for steaks.

A basic knowledge of the cooking times for all items on the menu contributes a great deal to "harmony" in the back *and* the front of the house. When you know that it takes 25 to 30 minutes to broil chicken, you won't start asking the chef for it after 15 minutes and you won't suggest it to the customer who says he/she is in a hurry!

Here are the approximate cooking times you should learn:

Chopped Sirloin:	20	Minutes
Filet Mignon:	20	"
New York Sirloin:	15	"
Club Sirloin:	20	"

Note: The above times are for "Medium." Figure more for "Well Done" and less for "Rare."

Broiled Ham Steak:	15	Minutes
Pork Chops:	25	"
Broiled Scallops:	15	"
Fried Scallops:	10	"
Broiled Lobster:	20	"
Boiled Lobster:	25	"
Fried Shrimp:	10	"
Baked Lobster:	20	"
Broiled Swordfish:	20	"

DAIRY, BREAD AND PASTRY PRODUCTS

Milk

The size of your restaurant and the volume of business you do, will dictate how you buy milk. It can be purchased in sizes ranging from 8 oz. containers to 5 or 10 gallon cans or plastic bags. A lot will depend on your refrigerator space and whether or not you have a milk dispenser.

With many people being diet conscious today, it would be well to have some low fat or skim milk available.

If you do not use the individual containers of Half and Half for coffee, you will need light cream for this, heavy cream for whipping (used on puddings, pies, etc.) and sour cream for baked potatoes.

Cheese

Your menu will dictate what kinds of cheese you will need in addition to American cheese (swiss cheese for Reuben sandwiches, cream cheese for sandwiches as well as some desserts, etc.). Go through your menu to find out if there are any other kinds you should have on hand.

Eggs

Buy only good, fresh eggs. The size purchased will be determined by what you intend to use them for.

Butter/Oleomargarine

If you use oleomargarine as a spread in place of butter, you are required, in most places, to note this on your menu. It is permissible to use oleo in cooking without noting the fact. Butter is scored, on a basis of 100 points, for five qualities—flavor, body, color, salt and packaging. The very best butter scores between 94 and 100. Butter scoring between 89 and 94 is good and does not have any off-taste or other objectionable features. Anything scoring below 89 would be apt to have an off-taste that customers might find offensive. I would suggest you use "93 Score" or better.

If you are operating a restaurant in an area where a good many of your customers are Jewish, they will expect unsalted butter.

Bread/Rolls

Bread for sandwiches comes in restaurant size loaves and you can get just about any kind in this size (white, wheat, rye, raisin, etc.). Only fresh bread should be used for sandwiches. Day old bread should be used for toast. Bread and rolls should be kept in a bread drawer, not left out in the kitchen, when not being used, and they must be wrapped tightly.

Rolls come in all sizes and shapes, sliced and unsliced, soft and hard. You will be purchasing the kinds your menu calls for: Dinner rolls (both soft and hard), large sandwich rolls for deli-type sandwiches (egg rolls, seeded and plain) as well as hamburger and frankfurter rolls. If your operation sells many hamburgers and frankfurters in rolls, it will save time to get these already sliced.

Pastry Products

If your operation is a small one (coffee shop, sandwich shop, small diner) it will not pay you to make your own cakes, pies, doughnuts. The cost of a baker and the necessary equipment (which would have to be figured into the space available in the kitchen) would make the cost prohibitive. Your best bet would be to find a wholesale baker who will furnish you with a *good* product—one which your customers will find acceptable.

FOOD PURCHASING

Your reputation is going to be built on the food you serve so it is important that you purchase fresh vegetables and fruits carefully and wisely. In large cities, there are always produce markets where you can pick out what you want, after checking condition, freshness and price of items. In smaller places, where there is no produce market nearby, you should be able to arrange with one of local supermarkets to supply you with fresh fruits and vegetables at lower prices than they charge their retail customers for the larger quantity you would need. In either case, here are a few examples of what you should look for:

Cabbage

Hard, solid heads that are heavy for their size. In addition to the regular variety, there is also Savoy cabbage (curly leaves) and red cabbage.

Lettuce

Three kinds of head lettuce are commonly used—Iceberg, Romaine and Leaf. They should be fresh, tender and crisp. The Iceberg and Romaine should be firm.

Celery

You can buy the whole stalk or celery hearts, depending on what they will be used for. They should break off easily, be of medium length and thickness and leaves should be fresh looking. Do not throw leaves or outer stalks away. They can be used in soups, stews or to flavor pot roast.

Potatoes

There are two types of potatoes. The mealy ones that are best for baking and mashing, and the harder type that are best for boiling and for other uses. Look for reasonably clean potatoes that are smooth skinned with shallow eyes (deep eyes mean too much waste). Avoid those that are soft or discolored and those with green tinged skin (apt to be bitter).

Peppers

These are divided into two types, those that are sweet and mild and those that are hot. The mild flavored ones are usually green or red (or they may have red streaks) and the hot peppers are always red. Buy only firm, smooth peppers. Size and shape are not that important unless you are planning to serve stuffed peppers, in which case you will want fairly large, well-shaped peppers.

Fresh Fruit

No matter which ones you are planning to buy, make sure they are not bruised or discolored. You want fruit that is fresh and not over-ripe so that it will keep for a few days without going bad.

Canned Foods

Canned foods of any kind are very practical, safe and ready to use without tying up your cook or your equipment. You want full value for your money which means you are interested in both quality and price. Today canned foods are guaranteed and there is a reliable way of identifying the quality inside each can. U.S. Grade A, B or C on the label means the product was processed and inspected by the Agricultural Marketing Service of the U.S. Department of Agriculture. You can choose Grade A (fancy), Grade B (choice) or Grade C (standard). With this system you can select the one that is best suited for whatever you will be using it for and the best one for the money you have to spend.

Commonly Used Dry Groceries

If you check the Purchasing Form in the "Menu Section" of this manual, you will find that there are many dry groceries that you will need in preparing your menu. The following may help you with your selection of some items, and the amounts to purchase.

Flour: If you will be making your own cakes and pies, you will want pastry flour which is milled from soft wheat, called weak flour; for breads you want a strong flour, which contains more gluten and less starch. All-purpose flour can be used for most kinds of baking and for making gravies and sauces.

Salt: Coarse and fine salt for cooking are both sold in bags. Buy iodized salt for table use as in some sections of the country there is a deficiency of iodine in food products.

Pepper: Use black pepper for table use (so customers can tell when they have used enough) but use white pepper for salads and in cooking.

Tea and Coffee: Buy the best, as many restaurants are judged by customers on the quality and taste of these two items. If possible purchase coffee in the bean and grind it to use.

Salad Oil: Buy polyunsaturated corn oil as it is odorless when used for frying, and other kinds may have an unpleasant odor. Many customers today are conscious of their cholesterol intake and the use of polyunsaturated fats helps to lower the cholesterol level.

Do not buy large large quantities of items that are subject to infestation by weevils or vermin unless you know they will be used up fairly quickly. Some of these are flour, dried fruit, cereals, spaghetti or macaroni products.

Poultry and Fish

Like pork, veal and lamb, poultry should always be well done. When buying chicken or turkey figure approximately three-quarters of a pound per serving as total weight of bird includes bones (which can be used to make soup along with wings, neck, etc.). A broiler will serve two people. *Turkey:* There is no difference in the meat quality of hen or tom turkeys, but the hen turkey usually has a wider breast. Young hens and toms are usually less than a year old, have softer meat and a flexible breast bone. Hens and toms that are more than a year old have tougher flesh and hardened breast bone. When purchasing look for fullness of the breast and under wings, as a well developed bird will yield more portions.

Chicken: You have a choice of several to choose from depending on the method of cooking. *Broilers:* Are young chickens of either sex which do not weigh over 2½ lbs. *Fryers:* These are the same as broilers but weigh between 2½ and 3½ lbs. *Roasters:* Also the same as broilers but weigh over 3½ lbs. *Capons:* Are unsexed male birds that weigh over 4 lbs. All of the above have soft meat and the capon is especially tender. *Fowls and Cocks:* Are mature female and male birds that can be of any size or weight and should only be used in stews and soups. *Fish:* Freshwater and saltwater fish differ in flavor and dryness of flesh, but there is no such thing as a tough fish so cook them carefully. With all fish it is important that you buy only the freshest as they deteriorate much more quickly than meat. The flesh should be firm, the odor fresh, skin and color bright and the body stiff. Fish fillets are a good buy as they are already skinned and boned. This gives you good portion control. Sole, haddock, cod and flounder are usually filleted when purchased. *Shell fish:* As with all fish, freshness is of utmost importance. If you haven't a good place to buy shellfish or other fish locally you would do well to buy it frozen. *Scallops:* The best are cream colored rather than white. Bay scallops are small, and sea scallops are much larger. They are soft, tender and a bit sticky from the juice. Do not wash them as it will change the flavor. *Shrimp:* They come in different sizes and are bought according to what they will be used for. Shrimp cocktail, salad, chop suey or baked, stuffed shrimp are some of most popular dishes. As with other fish, they have a special health value as they are rich in many body-building elements (calcium, copper, sulphur and phosphorus plus iodine). They also contain Vitamins A, B and D. *Clams:* There are soft and hard clams. The soft clam does not have as strong a flavor as the hard clam. They are usually used as "steamers" in New England clam chowder and fried. The hard clam comes in three sizes, the largest are used in chowders, the small hard clams known as Cherry- stones are served raw on the half-shell and the smallest are called Little Necks which are often eaten raw. *Oysters:* These will keep well if properly refrigerated. Properly chilled and kept at 32° they will keep upwards of three weeks, *but* at room temperature they will spoil in two days. *Do not* take any chances with them as they can cause serious illness.

YOUR BUSINESS IS FOOD

There are people in the restaurant business who never change their menu, style or decor. They are content to do just what they have been doing without trying any changes. If this is what you want, fine, but how much better for your customers, yourself and your profit to change your menu occasionally, change your color scheme, or the seating arrangements, if possible. You may find that even minor changes will improve your business. Keep it alive, interesting, different.

PORTION CONTROL

First I would suggest you reread the chapter in this manual entitled "Profit". There it says "profits do not just happen—they must be monitored and developed". One of the best ways to insure making a profit is to use portion control.

Your recipes should specify the number of servings per recipe, and you should be getting that number as this is what you have figured your cost on. For example if you have priced the pot roast figuring so many ounces per serving, if person doing the serving adds only one ounce to each plate—there goes the profit. If cook/chef has been told to use a No. 12 scoop for mashed potatoes and is using a No. 10 (which is larger) there goes your profit. This is true of all food served.

All personnel should be made aware of how important portion control is, and the owner/operator should make sure everyone is serving the proper sized portion.

When figuring the cost of a meal as served you must price every item included in the meal. You can figure on getting a certain number of servings from a pound or can of string beans, a loaf of bread, or a pound of bacon, but when it comes to beef, pork, lamb, etc. the cost per pound or per serving must be figured *after* it is trimmed and cooked, as the purchase price would include bones and fat and would not reflect any shrinkage that occurs during cooking.

Your profit comes *only* after food costs, fixed costs and other expenses are paid.

ICE CREAM DIPPING

Ideally, ice cream should be stored at 8 to 12 degrees Fahrenheit. Being a whipped product, it is full of air. When scooping ice cream, scoop it round—never dig or cut into the ice cream with the dipper. When you dig, you crush the light, airy texture of the ice cream which causes shrinkage in the yield. You get less servings per gallon when you don't scoop round. Be sure to use a dipper with a sharp edge that will cut into the ice cream cleanly. A scoop with a worn, dull edge will produce ragged-looking ice cream. The following chart will help you in figuring the portion size for your menu.

Scoop Size	Diameter of Scoop	Water wt. oz	Capacity fluid oz	Hamburger Patties per lb
6	3"	4.86	4.66	3
8	2-3/4"	3.80	3.64	3-1/2
10	2-5/8"	3.33	3.19	4
12	2-1/2"	2.90	2.78	5
16	2-1/4"	2.16	2.07	6–8
20	2-1/8"	1.84	1.77	9–10
24	2"	1.56	1.49	11–12
30	1-3/4"	1.07	1.03	13–14
40	1-1/2"	.64	.61	26
70	1-5/16"	.44	.42	36
100	1-1/8"	.28	.27	56

Remember, the bigger the scoop number, the smaller the size scoop. For example: A #100 size scoop is much smaller than a #12.

WINE SERVICE

A suitable wine enhances the enjoyment of a meal. Although wine is steadily increasing in popularity, most people know little about wine service. Consequently, a guest may be reluctant to order it. You don't have to be a continental wine steward to do this successfully. These simple rules will assist you.

Some customers will know just what wine they want with their meal and will usually order a brand name. Employees should be ready and able to help those who may ask for advice or suggestions. If they are having any kind of fish or white meat a white wine, such as Chablis or Sauterne, should be recommended. Burgundy or Port (red wines) should be suggested if they are having lamb, red meat or game. If it is a special occasion (wedding, anniversary, birthday, etc.) Champagne or Sparkling Burgundy would be a good selection.

Employees should learn a few names at a time in each classification, in order to become more knowledgeable and therefore more helpful to the customers.

An ice bucket is used to chill sparkling, white and rosé wines before they are served in chilled glasses.

Wines to be served at room temperature (still red wines) may be served from a wine basket.

The bartender will usually loosen corks on wine bottles so they can be easily removed at the table before serving. A napkin should be held over top of bottle until cork is pulled. Top of bottle should be wiped off both before and after cork is removed.

Before pouring, show the label to the person who did the ordering so they know they are getting what they asked for.

The correct serving of wine helps add a festive note to dining out. It should not be hurried. First a little of the wine is poured for the one who ordered. When it has been tasted and approval is given, the other glasses are then poured and more wine is added to the taster's glass. Turn the bottle to the right after pouring to prevent any wine from being spilled. After pouring return bottle to ice bucket and cover with a napkin to help keep it cool. A side towel should be used when pouring wine. It is not necessary to refill the glasses unless asked to do so.

There is apt to be sediment in the bottom of bottles of red wine so do not use last few drops.

Wine and beer sales can greatly increase your profits.

DRAUGHT BEER

There are two types of beer you can sell if you have a license to do so—bottled and draught. Customer acceptability and cost will help you determine which to sell. If you check the cost for a half barrel of draught beer and figure out how many glasses you can get from one (depending on size of glass) you will most likely find it to be more profitable than bottled beer. The following will give you an approximate estimate of what you should expect to get out of a half barrel.

The Approximate returns in terms of glasses and income from a Half Barrel of Beer*

	8 oz.	10 oz.	12 oz.	14 oz.
No. of glasses—no foam	248	198	165	141
No. of glasses—20% foam	292	234	196	161
Income no waste 20% foam @ .35	102.20	81.90	68.60	58.10
Income no waste 20% foam @ .40	116.80	93.60	78.40	66.40
Income no waste 20% foam @ .45	131.40	105.30	88.20	74.70
Income no waste 20% foam @ .50	146.00	117.00	98.00	83.00
Income no waste 20% foam @ .55	160.60	128.70	107.80	91.30

*This is based on a half barrel containing approximately 15 ½ gallons. A 20% collar represents about a ¾ inch head.

SUMMARY: Your personnel should be made aware of above chart and should be checked to make sure they are charging correct price for size of glass used.

Draught or bottled beer should be served very cold.

Beer service like wine service will greatly increase profitability of your operation.

PICKING UP THE ORDER

Picking up the order requires a technique as well as a knowledge of cooking time.

In picking up "starters" be sure to pick up the cold ones first, and hot soups last, using soup covers when available.

Never pick up for two tables unless it is for the two's, two singles or a two and a single.

Possibility of Food Shortages

As of this writing growers of food face a possible power shortage which will affect water supplies. This could hit the food service operator hard in getting food supplies by distributors, processors, growers and manufacturers. Fuel shortages will also affect the above mentioned group. Many distributors are changing their trucks over from gas to diesel power and getting much better mileage. The cost of diesel fuel is no longer that much cheaper than gas but its mileage yield is much better.

Distributors are going more and more for the "one stop" concept of selling food service operators all of their needs. The increased cost of operating and maintaining vehicles is making more distributors go this one stop route. Some are also imposing minimum dollar requirements for deliveries.

Cold storage is also being hard hit due to the high cost of utility power. I feel, that in spite of this, you will not see the cost of gasoline affect sales in the food service industry. Eating out is now a way of life for many people. It is done at work, at school and in different groups. We do it for excitement and pleasure and at different times throughout the day. It's something we all do. What increasing utility costs are going to mean is that owners and managers are going to have to be better business people and come up with ways to offset the rising operating costs of doing business. They will all have to do this to insure a profit in order to stay in business.

Fast Foods

Europeans are now copying our fast food concept in food service; i.e. counters, snack bars, coffee shops, doughnut shops, etc.

Cafeterias—Counters

This type of operation goes back many years. Although in some places, New England for example, cafeterias are not that popular, counters are an American tradition and are seen throughout the country.

Restaurant—Cart Service

Carts with side heater units that are pushed to the table are slowly dying away. The customer is not willing to pay for the extra service. The knowledgeable operator who knows how to run this type of restaurant is fast disappearing.

Table Service

This is more American than most types. The food is served from the left and taken away from the right. It is put on plates in the kitchen and carried in to be served at the table.

English Service

This is similar to the American style except the food is put on the tables in serving dishes and on platters for the guests to help themselves, or the waiter/waitress may go around to serve what is requested the first time and then leave the rest of food on the table. You will find this is done for large groups in some restaurants.

French Service

For showmanship and to attract the attention of other diners the plate is made up at table side, or the finishing is done in front of the customer. This is usually a more leisurely meal and a quick turnover is not expected.

QUESTIONS

1. It is usually safest to buy daily needs on a monthly basis.

   True ____   False ____

2. What should the supplier know before making a delivery?

3. What are five procedures involved in receiving an order?

4. What is an incoming delivery report used for?

5. What should be done with swollen cans of fruit, vegetables or other food items?

6. Why should food items and nonfood items be kept separate in any accounting?

7. What is a perpetual inventory sheet used for?

8. What are the advantages of portion control items?

9. What are the advantages of having a low inventory?

8
Equipment, Design and Decor

Once you have formed your menu you must then see that the food is delivered, stored, prepared and served in the most efficient way possible. This means installing proper equipment and arranging it in such a way that the work can flow quickly and smoothly even at the busiest hours.

The restaurant's seating capacity should be as large as is comfortably possible, and flexible enough to handle different sized groups of people. The decor should express the theme of the restaurant and communicate your special concept to the customers.

EQUIPMENT

The following are points you should consider in purchasing and arranging your equipment:

1. In the late sixties the cost for electricity and gas was approximately 1 percent of gross sales; now it is approximately 8–10 percent and who knows what it will be in the future? Due to shrinking gas supplies, more and more owners will be using electricity. Thoughtful decisions on your part will keep energy costs from eating up your profit.

2. Consider using vertical space in arranging equipment, for instance double decker ovens, etc.

3. Most heavy equipment has a life expectancy of 10 years.

4. Show off your new equipment to customers.

5. Who will train employees to use the equipment? Will you have time?

6. Visualize the equipment. Draw it out on paper. Look at the menu and visualize the work flow in the kitchen at busy times. When it's busy and you need dishwasher rack storage, will you have enough room? When the sandwich board area is busy is there enough room for two people to work side by side? How many orders of toast can you make at once?

7. Select equipment which is sanitation-approved nationally. It is easy to clean and can be rolled away to enable staff to clean behind it.

8. Microwave ovens, convection ovens and other types of special equipment have been developed in recent years, but never buy a piece of equipment unless its usefulness (to you) justifies the cost. Talk to other restaurant owners who are using a new type of equipment and find out how they like it.

9. Consider your employees—good lighting, ventilation, and kitchen equipment and work surfaces at a proper height in the work area will improve morale.

10. Grill area can be in front. Customers welcome open view preparation areas.

11. Purchase known brand name standard equipment. Keep instruction books for each piece of equipment covering use, care and repair information. Your restaurant supply company will give them to you on a no-charge basis.

12. Do not stock up on backup pots, pans, flatware, etc. Let the restaurant supply house stock the equipment—that is their business, your business is food. Extra equipment that is not in use has a tendency to disappear. Be sure you keep track of all items large and small.

13. When wiring for electrical equipment, be sure to allow for future equipment you may want to install.

14. Get more than one price before you contract with a restaurant supply house, designer or restaurant consultant. Be sure to tell them your objectives, problems and financial resources. Their ideas can save you a lot of time and money, but they must have a true understanding of your wishes and resources.

15. Have you a plan for an alternate source of power if you are in an area where storms could knock out your electricity?

16. Storeroom shelving is normally 6–7 feet high and 24 inches deep. This is more than adequate to handle cases of food products and supplies.

17. Regarding layout—consider how many steps the employee has to take in order to serve the item. What is the body motion required? How strenuous is the operating of the equipment?

18. Heavily used pieces of equipment should be the most accessible.

19. Equipment must be placed in accordance with health, fire and safety codes and regulations.

20. Consider accessibility of equipment for repairs, maintenance and cleaning.

21. Equipment needing water must be situated near a sink.

22. Ovens need nearby benches to hold large pots and pans while cooling.

23. Discourage "divorced operations" where food is prepared downstairs and served upstairs, it is too costly in terms of both money and efficiency.

24. Estimate the number of people you have to serve and the time you have in which to serve them.

25. How near is the storeroom to the equipment?

26. Keep equipment in good repair to eliminate costly breakdowns.

27. Set up pickup stations in order of need; appetizer, soup, coffee, desserts, etc. Strive for efficiency and step-saving layout to improve waiter/waitress performance.

28. A 30" work aisle is acceptable in most operations. The kitchen aisle should be at least 40" in areas where equipment is giving off heat.

29. Door openings should be large enough to bring equipment through—both the equipment you have today and that you may want at a future time.

30. Allow for cost of installation and operation of water cooled motors.

31. Before purchasing equipment know what services the supplier will perform. Will they train your employees in its proper use? Will they service equipment? Will they provide a substitute, in case of a breakdown, to avoid tie-up time?

China is usually purchased on a ratio of 2½ times the seating capacity. It is less for items not frequently used.

Other things to consider when purchasing china:

The type of business you open will determine what kind of china will be used. If you open a coffee shop or a luncheonette you may use a mug for serving coffee, tea and hot chocolate. If you open a more formal restaurant (fancy tablecloths, rugs on the floor, paintings on the wall, etc.) you will want to serve coffee from stainless steel pots and you will use cups and saucers.

Will your dealer be ordering this china especially for you or is it in stock? This is very important when you go to order replacements.

Purchasing china is a big investment and, as owner/operator, you must remember that if you pick a certain style and color to match your walls, curtains or rugs you may have a problem when you want to change color or style of any of these things. When you make your initial purchase pick a color and style of china that will go with anything.

Restaurant china because of the way it is made will keep hot food hot and cold food cold.

China can be your silent partner in promoting your menu.

HOW TO PREVENT CHINA BREAKAGE

1. A well laid out kitchen with the proper work flow and a place for everything can help keep breakage to a minimum.

2. Having big enough soiled dish tables to hold all the dirty dishes, even during peak periods.

3. Separating glasses, dishes and silverware before they go to the dish attendant.

4. Use of proper mobile carts and bus boxes.

5. Stock levels must be supervised by the owner/operator during busy periods. When service people are rushed during a peak period and run short of plates, cups, saucers, etc. the tendency is to rush everything (including china) to the dish attendant to be washed. Then it is rushed back to the service area. This is a sure way to end up with some broken china.

6. Food service equipment dealers and detergent companies can offer many suggestions for the layout of dishwashing facilities

or for the improvement of existing dishroom facilities. Many will also train your personnel in the proper methods and use of a dish machine.

USING CHINA TO PROMOTE YOUR MENU

You can use china to help merchandise your menu by the use of different shapes, colors, patterns for special occasions. I remember one restaurant where all fish items on Fridays were served on fish-shaped china.

You can develop your menu to its fullest by appealing to the customers' sense of sight before appealing to their sense of taste.

The use of such items as demitasse cups, escargot plates, egg cups, etc. will also help promote your menu.

DESIGN AND DECOR

Your restaurant concept expressed through your design and decor, must catch the customer's interest. The fastmoving, car-driving, restaurant-sophisticated public must see something on the outside of your building which will encourage them to stop.

The waiting customer should have something enjoyable to do once he/she is inside the restaurant. For this reason many restaurants provide a cocktail lounge and a system for adding this charge to the customer's dinner check. The waiting (or vestibule) area can be used to display posters advertising special functions, the menu, the hours you are open, etc. These are things your customers can read while they are waiting to be seated.

In planning the seating area you must allow for different types of seating arrangements: booths, standard tables which can be separated or pushed together, stools, etc. Twelve square feet is usually allowed per customer, and up to 16 square feet for a restaurant with a high check average. Booths are the most popular type of seating, but are not always the most efficient, as two people will often choose to sit in a four-person booth and there is not much you can do to offset this. Deuce tables are popular as they can accommodate two people, or many when they are put together. The four-seaters are popular for your family trade. If your restaurant has an attractive view, try to seat as many people facing it as possible. Remember to include coat racks and baby chairs in your dining area.

A reputable manufacturer or equipment company can be a big help in assisting you with the seating layout. They can suggest how to get maximum seating, and show you how to place seating around beams, low windows, etc. They also can give you great suggestions on how to deal with vestibules or reception areas so you can accommodate 10 to 15 people all arriving at once, and not interfere with people leaving. Take advantage of their years in the business.

To give you an idea of the square feet needed per seat use the following guide:

Type of Restaurant	Approximate Size Needed
High Type: Table service	16 square feet
Regular: Cafeteria	14 square feet
Short order	11–12 square feet
Table service	14 square feet
Banquets	8–10 square feet

Your seating arrangement can be used to calculate your potential income. Multiply the average check, say $3.00, times the seating capacity, say 100, times the turnover, say 3 times, and you have an idea of what your income could be during a given time period ($900.00). This same calculation can be used throughout the day, but you must adjust the figures to reflect the number of seats actually in use.

LAYOUT

When you lay out a kitchen in your restaurant correctly it keeps morale of employees high and also keeps the payroll in line. A logical layout will save food cost, and help make for a successful business.

Let's consider other factors to look for in the layout.

By now, you should know the number of people you can serve and the time it will take to serve them. Look at the menu and match it to your equipment and the necessary preparation time.

You may ask if there is a special formula to follow in laying out your restaurant? I say *no*, but some people will differ, and give you certain rules of thumb to follow. However, to say each layout should be the same is not true. It depends on the size and shape of the room (square, rectangular, etc.) and other considerations unforeseen by anyone in the planning stage.

Each case presents its own set of problems.

SUGGESTION

Many people try to act as their own contractors and this can cause some serious problems unless the owner/operator understands exactly what to do. Get help or hire someone to do it. If you do act as your own contractor, more often than not you will eventually have to hire someone to finish what was started incorrectly, which will make for unnecessary cost.

GENERAL INFORMATION

We mentioned earlier how to make a layout of equipment on paper. One very simple method involves taking a large sheet of paper and the list of equipment you need. Reduce it to ¼" or ½" on small strips of paper. Label each strip by using colored dots to represent grill, stove, sink, etc. and see if you feel the flow of equipment relates to the person actually working that piece of equipment. Equate it to ease of operation and movability. Consider also how electricity, gas and water will get to these pieces of equipment.

Make general section headings, i.e. cashier section, restrooms, storeroom, parking lot, and list their needs. You will be surprised at all the things you will find that *are* needed to run a profitable operation, and you will be equally surprised at all the things people *say* you need that you can do without.

PHYSICAL BUILDING PROBLEMS

Consideration should be given to handicaps such as beams, low cellars, drafts from doorways, doors that open into areas you can not see easily (for security reasons), etc.

LAYOUT FLOW ROUTE–1

Take your menu and follow what must happen to each item. For instance in the kitchen, once the bowl is taken off the mixer and must be washed, how many steps must be taken? While the pot is on the mixer and water is needed, how far away is the sink? Is the dishroom arranged so when it is busy there is room to stack the dirty dishes without breakage?

LAYOUT FLOW ROUTE–2

The ideal flow pattern is as follows: Receiving, storage, prepreparation, preparation. We said the location of important "by-need" items was important. A work table and slicer should be near a refrigerator, vegetable steamers near sinks, and mixers near water. In a one-person kitchen the refrigerator should be located near the broiler with a sink and a work table between the refrigerator and sink.

SPECIAL RAMP FOR WHEEL CHAIRS

This service to wheel chair custômers is deeply appreciated by all. You would be using good business judgment in installing a special ramp for these customers and have rest room facilities to meet their needs, also as relates to special equipment needs.

COMMENTS ON DO'S AND DON'TS

I relate all the do's and don'ts and formula charts to football. Every coach tells his players that each play is designed to produce a touchdown, but in the actual games every play called doesn't produce a touchdown. Why not? Because something went wrong, or something had to give. The same holds true in laying out a restaurant. It is important you should know why it should be done and how it should be done to obtain the 100 percent perfection each time which you are striving for.

DINING ROOM

One helpful hint I would like to pass along: If you have sizable seating capacity in a dining room, consider the distance the waiter/

waitress has to walk from the point of serving. If the distance to be covered is considerable cold foods may become warm and hot foods may become cool. Ideally the food preparation area should be as close as possible to the service points, and to every seat in the restaurant.

TIME AND ENERGY SAVING EQUIPMENT

Stay abreast of factors that will help you do the job faster, easier, better, and will help justify the cost of the equipment. For example, fluorescent light bulbs are being made with less overall output, a timer can shut off equipment when it reaches the set temperature, devices on motors monitor their performance, making sure they are running as they should. All these save energy and make for better functionable equipment. These are things you must consider. You will also see companies working on devices that will help cut down on high energy bills. Keep informed as to what is available to you. There will be a lot of changes in the near future.

EQUIPMENT REPLACEMENT

Many times the question is asked "How often should one replace equipment or change decor? What is the life expectancy of heavy equipment?".

I suggest that you evaluate your business in 5 to 6 years and consider whether or not to change the decor at that point, if your business image is still acceptable and you can afford it. If you come to the conclusion that you are offering a concept that is no longer appealing to the public, you must look at the possibility of changing the image altogether, rather than just refurbishing a somewhat successful one.

The life expectancy of heavy equipment is 10 years.

You can get advice from knowledgeable people in equipment, design and decor to give your restaurant a unique atmosphere and personality which will bring people back again and again. The important things that make any layout work are interested employees who are properly motivated, and knowledgeable management that stays in tune with the business and knows what is going on at all times.

This section is intended to acquaint you with the various basic and most popular items in the restaurant industry today. Your menu dictates your equipment needs.

There are many different kinds of ranges, ovens, fryers, steam kettles, steam cookers, mixers, etc. on the market. They differ in size, design and floor space used.

The type of restaurant you have, the number of customers you can accommodate, the size of your kitchen and what your cooking requirements are, will determine what equipment you will need.

You will not need the largest, heaviest equipment if you only have a small restaurant. The heavy duty ranges, battery operations (which are oven, range, fryer, etc. assembled as one unit) are necessary for large restaurants, hotels or hospitals, but are definitely not required for the small or medium-sized operation that most readers of this book will be interested in.

Check out the brand names that you are familiar with, ones that you have seen used in other restaurants, or those that have been recommended to you as being appropriate in your type of business by someone knowledgeable in this field. Mongrel equipment, or an unknown piece of equipment, is apt to cost you more in the long run. It may be hard to get service or parts. The known brands have a reputation to uphold, so you can be sure of getting good service when needed, and you can rely on parts being readily available. Mongrel equipment can be best explained by a company selling a piece of equipment that takes odd size pans which are hard to find; chopping blades which are not standard to the industry. Such a company may discontinue making those special pans and you, the owner/operator, will have a piece of equipment that you can't find replacement pans or parts for.

Whether or not you use gas or electric equipment depends not only on your preference but on availability and cost in your area.

Before you buy any piece of equipment determine its true value to you—how much faster can you produce an item by using it? Is the quality of item changed by using this piece of equipment? Can you get replacement parts and follow-up service? Are you getting good quality for the price you are paying? Can you afford the item in question?

Most food service equipment manufacturers produce excellent, long lasting products, but it would be wise to check with two or three companies regarding price, quality, and service along with the other considerations previously mentioned.

The life expectancy of any piece of equipment will be determined in good part by how well you maintain it. Most restaurant equipment is used many hours a day *nonstop*. It is worthwhile to keep it in good condition because breakdowns on evenings, holidays or weekends can be very costly.

GENERAL INFORMATION

The following are the most common basic needs in a restaurant. This is merely a guide, as needs differ from restaurant to restaurant.

Scales

For receiving (known as platform scales).
For measuring (known as counter or kitchen scales).

Grills or Broilers

For open face cooking.
Griddle plates are often used.

Coffee Makers

Many types are available. Check on the water pressure in your area.

Steam Tables

Be concerned with top arrangement. What type of pans, pots can be arranged in it?
This is a must for any good-sized restaurant.

Microwave Oven

Check oven cavity for size of pan it will take.
Check types of timers. Can it thaw food conveniently?
Compare different makes.

Mixers

A mixer is a must for almost any size restaurant. They come in various sizes.
They are available with different speeds which is important, (to prevent splashing).

Slicers

Check for quality construction.
Get one that can be used for slicing anything from tomatoes to hot and cold meat.
Many features are available in different makes.

Toasters

Many types to choose from.
Available in stands and with bread sleeves if desired.

Wire Shelving

Much needed throughout any restaurant.

Refrigerator

Check for construction, guarantees, lighting, tray slides, capacity, etc.
Compare different makes and models.

Dishwasher

Check construction inside and out.
Compare different makes and models.

Fryers

Check construction.
Compare different makes and models for capacity and heat controls.

Walk-in Coolers

There are many types and sizes. Compare.

Sinks

These come in various sizes.
Check for construction inside and out.
Inside corners have different arrangements. By this I mean a sink can be square cornered or coved, meaning half rounded. It is easier to clean a coved cornered sink, and there is less possibility of dirt accumulating in a coved cornered sink vs. a square cornered sink.

Food Chopper (also called a Buffalo Chopper)

Has many attachments available.
An excellent piece of equipment that will save you money if you have the need for it.

Drink Dispensers (see-through)

Effective sales tool.
Must be kept clean.

Open-Face Burner

There are many kinds to choose from. Compare.

Sandwich Units

Come in various sizes all having many different features.

Heating Lamps

Excellent for keeping fast-moving items ready.

EQUIPMENT NEEDS

The following list can be used as a reminder of equipment needed for various operations:

Diner type Operation

Cook's Table
Scales
Toaster
Hood with Exhaust
Air-cooling System
Mixers
Fryers
Coffee Urn/Coffee Machine
Sandwich Unit
Griddle
Dishroom Accessories
Slicer
Garbage Disposal
Steam Table
Pot and Vegetable Sink
Dishwasher w/Drain Board
Food Choppers
Meat Block or Board
Refrigerator and Freezer

If you plan any type of baking on the premises you will have to consider the following:

Dough Divider
Proof Boxes
Stack Ovens
Cooling Racks
Trays and Pans
Pastry Bags
Doughnut Machine
Display Cases

Coffee or Sandwich Shop

Register
Coffee Brewer
Broiler—Griddle
Fryer

Milk Machine
Hood and Exhaust
Display Cases
Sinks
Ice Machine
Refrigerators/Freezer
Cream Dispenser
Ice Cream holding unit
Small Equipment Accessories
Toaster
Scales
Meat Grinder (Chopper)
Outdoor Needs (Signs, Landscaping, etc.)

CARE AND CLEANING OF EQUIPMENT

Equipment costs money and in order to keep it in good repair and working condition it is the responsibility of the owner/operator and person using the equipment to see that it is properly used and taken care of. It should give years of dependable service if it has been properly installed and used correctly as per manufacturer's instructions. A representative from the manufacturer is usually present after the installation to give instructions to those who will be using each piece of equipment. If directions are followed as to use and cleaning it will help keep repairs to a minimum.

Electrical Cooking Equipment

After the equipment has been installed it must be inspected by fire underwriters, who will determine its safety.

Today, with fuel costs so high, it is imperative that each piece of equipment be used as efficiently as possible. Electrical appliances, unlike gas, continue heating for a period, after being turned off, so operator should take this into consideration. This is one way to save and to also make sure item being prepared is not overcooked.

The owner/operator should check these appliances periodically and make sure they are being kept clean, are being oiled as per manufacturer's manual and that heat controls are working properly.

If you can make an arrangement with a service firm to come in on a regular basis, they will check each piece of equipment and make sure everything is in good working order. Here is a partial list of things to check for:

1. Plugs fit properly (are not loose or cracked).
2. Cords are not frayed, twisted or otherwise not in good condition. Frayed cords can cause a fire and they should be *replaced* not repaired.
3. If a piece of equipment is not working, did the fuse box get checked? It may only require a new fuse.
4. An electrician can repair broken wires in electrical heating units, which would save buying a new unit.
5. Are all electrical wires and elements free from grease and dust. If not, clean them right away.
6. When using water to clean around electrical equipment, make sure no water gets into heating element. This is dangerous as any dampness or moisture can cause a short circuit and this could start a fire.

If anyone of the above problems cannot be taken care of by you or your personnel, call it to the attention of the service people when they come.

Gas-operated Cooking Equipment

Here again, the fire underwriters will determine if all safety requirements have been met (re: installation and performance).

Gas cooking equipment should be set on a raised, fireproof platform (this helps keep underparts from being corroded when floor is washed or when water is spilled).

Grease in ducts and under hoods can cause a fire. They should be cleaned at regular intervals and, at least once a year, the equipment should be dismantled and cleaned thoroughly by a firm that will also coat the inside of the ducts with a fireproof substance.

A ventilating system should be installed under the hood (usually included with the hood) to draw off smoke and cooking odors.

As with electrical equipment, use each appliance as efficiently as possible as this will make it more productive and also reduce fuel costs.

Regular maintenance for this equipment is needed to keep it in best possible condition. A service firm or plumber can be hired to do this work (some gas companies will also do this for a nominal fee). They should:

1. Check pilot light and flame in each burner. A clear blue flame shows you are getting proper mix of gas and air.
2. Make sure oven temperature and dial of thermostat check out the same. If they don't the product in oven could end up undercooked or overcooked.
3. Valves should be easy to use otherwise they should be lubricated.

To keep your equipment in good working order for a long period, and to get good results from it, you must make sure that the operator is using it properly by:

1. Using correct temperature, as anything higher than needed causes product to shrink and is wasteful.
2. Using ovens when possible so top of range is not overloaded.
3. Not turning equipment on when they come in if it will not be used until much later. Also turning it off when not in use.

Refrigerator and Freezer Appliances

No special training is required for day to day maintenance of refrigerator or freezer. This can be taken care of by owner/manager or by one of the employees who has been instructed in what needs to be done.

1. Manufacturer's manual will tell you how to lubricate compressor motors. Use only amount and grade of oil they recommend.
2. Most units today do not have to be defrosted. If you have one that does require defrosting, do not let ice build up in freezer or on coils as this cuts down on efficiency. Defrost as often as necessary to keep it in the best possible working condition.
3. Door gaskets should be soft, not stiff and brittle. Put a piece of paper between door and unit. If it can be pulled out easily the gaskets need replacing.

4. Check bolts that are holding motor. Tighten if necessary. Vibration when motor is running may cause them to loosen which causes more vibration.
5. Do not open doors unnecessarily or leave them open any longer than necessary.
6. Use vacuum or stiff brush on compressor motor every week to remove dust.
7. If you ever suspect a refrigerator leak call your service company at once.
8. Keep thermometers in both refrigerators and freezer. Watch temperatures to make sure they stay at proper levels.

The equipment manual, and your service company, will advise you about other points you should check to avoid any serious problems or a breakdown.

All equipment having motors and/or moving parts needs to be lubricated at regular intervals. Check your manual to see when, where and how often this should be done and what kind or grade of oil to use. One person should be responsible for seeing that this is done.

Scales

The "Bureau of Standards" in your city is supposed to make periodic check of all scales in stores and restaurants, to make sure they are accurate. You may call them if you feel that yours are not.

Convection, Baking and Roasting Ovens

Various types and sizes available.
Compare and buy according to your needs.

Energy-Saving Tips:

1. Check the BTU rating for window air-conditioners. The higher the number—the more efficient the unit. (Note: BTU stands for British thermal unit and is the quantity of heat required to raise the temperature of one pound of water one degree Fahrenheit.)

2. When planning a new facility consider adding a vestibule. This will help keep temperature constant in the dining area.

3. At closing time make sure all kitchen equipment, blowers, air-conditioners, etc. have been turned off. All lights should be turned off except those left on for security reasons.

4. Light bulbs are not operating efficiently when they start to dim. Replace them.

5. When choosing paint for walls remember that pale colors reflect light.

6. Fluorescent bulbs are more efficient than the standard incandescent bulbs when used indoors.

7. When you open business for the day don't turn equipment on to the highest setting.

8. Food is not cooked any faster by turning burner to highest point. It just uses more energy.

9. Use plate covers (or cook with covers) so food doesn't cool off as this would necessitate reheating.

10. Slow cooking saves the most energy.

11. Allow enough clearance in ovens for air to circulate around pans.

12. Turn equipment off when it is not being used.

13. Don't leave dishwasher running when not in use.

14. If you use gas equipment make sure gas flame is blue with a firm-looking center. A yellow tip means gas is escaping.

15. Keep steam tables covered but don't have temperature so high that steam is escaping. This will only result in over-cooked food.

16. Check the calibration of ovens, fryers, etc. with the thermostat reading.

17. Make sure all equipment has breathing space and is kept clean.

18. Close doors as soon as possible after putting anything in or taking anything out of refrigerators or freezers.

SUMMARY: A basic listing is what we have given you. The food service equipment industry is a big business. When making a major equipment purchase, consider the following:

1. What kind of a track record does the company in question have for selling this type of equipment?

2. Do they have the means to deliver, install and hook up the equipment?
3. Will they service the equipment for repairs?
4. Do they have parts in stock if they are needed?
5. Check the guarantee on equipment, ease of cleaning, power usage and various other accessories. Compare different companies.
6. Is the equipment you need in stock or must it be ordered? How long will you have to wait for delivery?
7. Select only equipment that will last. You get this knowledge by getting free cut-out sheets from your restaurant equipment company. Compare and talk to people who are using the same type of equipment and get their opinions on particular brands.

Two of the biggest mistakes you can make are (1) to buy an oversized piece of equipment you really don't need, or (2) to buy an inferior piece of equipment.

QUESTIONS

1. Equipment needs are determined by what four factors?

2. What is the major factor in determining the life expectancy of a piece of equipment?

3. Every restaurant should have heavy duty range and battery operation unit.

    True ____   False ____

4. Mongrel brands of equipment are just as good as the well-known brands.

    True ____   False ____

5. The true value of a piece of equipment is determined by what factors?

6. What are the two biggest mistakes made in buying equipment?

7. Most heavy equipment will last 20 or 30 years with proper use.

    True ____   False ____

8. What is meant by the "proper flow" of equipment?

9. China is usually purchased on a ratio of ___ times the seating capacity.

10. What is the area usually allowed, per customer, for

   a. a restaurant with high check average?

   ___

   b. a banquet?

   ___

11. Where should the work table be located in a one-person kitchen?

12. Name two examples of time and energy saving equipment.

9
Profit

In this section we will discuss profit: How to obtain it, what to watch for, ways to insure a profit, danger signals to look for to pre-warn you to change your course of direction, plus other helpful information. If you reread these points they will be most beneficial to you for many years to come.

In a restaurant you will find your profit comes in slowly. The reason for this lies in the fact that you must constantly replenish food and supplies, and there are continuing expenses for which money must always be ready—for example, payroll, rent, operating expenses, plus the unexpected expenses, a broken drain, a leaking roof, a piece of equipment that cannot be repaired.

What is the percentage of profits as it relates to your sales? Your percentage of profits to sales runs between 6–12 percent. In prac-tical terms this means that in order for you to take $15,000.00 out of the business yearly, your business must gross $125,000.00 per year—12 percent of which would yield you the $15,000.00. As you can see, the percentage of profit as it relates to your sales is not a very big figure. Profits do not just happen, they must be *monitored, developed* and worked at always. For example, a business has a potential, and the owner/operator must either be satisfied to keep it at its current level, or he/she must decide how best to im-prove it and set a higher potential of sales and profit for the business. This can be done through new menus with higher check average, increased seating capacity and higher unit sales, to list a few.

Since money is constantly needed in a restaurant to meet the demands previously listed, it is very important that accurate records are maintained, and that through them a constant watch is kept on expenses. You cannot commit yourself to paying bills, or to buying goods, and *hope* the money will come in from increased business or predicate the amount of money you spend, on anything but tangible factors.

For example, you are the owner/operator of a restaurant. You employ eight waiters/waitresses and operate a drive-in type of business. You read in the newspaper that the road directly in front of your place of business is going to be under construction for approximately 6 months. Here is a situation you must react to and watch closely. You may find that once construction starts business may fall off sharply, therefore you cannot afford to maintain the same work force. You may find you have to adjust your payroll and operating costs to meet the situation. This is what is called reacting to the problem. Before you cut your employees' work time, however, think out the situation. Possibly, with all the workers on the street, your business may not be affected. You may find that putting out a different type of menu to satisfy their appetites will keep you operating in the black. The important thing is to be ready to act if you have to, when and if sales drop. They always drop faster it seems than they go up, and if you are not ready ahead of time to adjust your operating costs, you will be in trouble.

Another problem area to watch out for, is food supplies. If you agree to pay $1.75 a pound for meat, you assume that the meat coming in will be priced at $1.75 a lb. You could be sadly mistaken. Make it a point to check the bill and be certain the price you agreed to pay is the price you are being charged.

At one time or another you will hear the term "breakeven". It is merely the point at which gross profit dollars equal expenses: For example:

Sales	$100,000.00	
Cost of Goods	60,000.00	
Expenses–Controlled		These two expenses equal
and Uncontrolled	40,000.00	what you have taken in
		sales.

Taking into consideration the operating cost of expenses (both controlled and uncontrolled) $100,000.00 is not showing a profit, but it has broken even.

What must this business do to insure a profit? Once you have discovered what the profit factor is, and, through analysis of current sales and through increased projections, you feel that this business can, let us say, gross $175,000.00, you must control cost to be certain a profit will exist. To insure a profitable year and to live with the incoming sales (based on what you forecast for the various items in controlled and uncontrolled expenses) either sales must increase without operating costs increasing drastically, or costs must be reduced.

Remember that cutting costs does not always mean cutting employees' hours and all other types of expenses. Better productivity from employees, increased sales, improving operational methods, etc, can all be factors which can produce a better profit for you.

PROFIT THROUGH BUDGETING

Learn how to budget time for jobs to be done. For example, if you need six waitresses, each working 8 hours per day, think in terms of 48 hours per day times what you will be paying them per day—this will equal your dollar payroll cost for waitresses for one day. Breaking down each group in that way you will have learned what is needed in hours for each person, and you will be able to control hours worked more efficiently.

Budget the expenses of the following items both daily and weekly:

Food	Menus
Payroll	Laundering
Maintenance	Uniforms
Repairs (estimate)	Local promotion
Supplies	Advertising
China/Glassware	Rent
Silverware	Insurance

Make it a part of your job to know what the rent is per day, the telephone cost per day, the payroll per day, food cost per day. Think of it in terms of *dollars*.

PROFITS THROUGH SECURITY

1. Be sure you collect for all that is served.
2. Check receiving of all goods.
3. Watch where employees park their cars, as previously mentioned, make sure it's not near the back door.
4. Issue keys to certain people only and hold them responsible for the safety of those keys. Make sure no one makes a duplicate set of keys for their own use.
5. Observe employees' packages going in and out.
6. Control employees' meals.
7. Make sure delivery and salespeople (all visitors) check with the manager or owner before going into the stockroom, office or other places that should be off limits.

PROFIT THROUGH TURNOVER

Many successful restaurant operators store only a week's supply of inventory. By doing this you tie up less capital, insure proper stock rotation and have less chance of pilferage, spoilage and hidden or misplaced items.

Keep your source of supply in mind—how far are they from you? In case of an emergency, how soon can they deliver? Will you be able to pick it up?

PROFIT THROUGH WEEKLY FORECAST

After approximately 2 months of operation, having logged in daily sales, daily number of meals sold, daily cost, special weather conditions and events, you will be able to see a pattern developing whereby you can project your purchasing and payroll needs down pretty well. In the beginning this will be difficult because you do not know how the menu will be accepted, and you will still be finding out about likes and dislikes in the area.

PROFIT THROUGH INVENTORY CONTROL

Use your storeroom control sheets. Date and price each item (all #10 cans, bags of flour, etc.). You will find this to be an excellent way of assuring a profit and will help make employees aware of how much things cost.

PROFIT THROUGH PERPETUAL INVENTORY

Use your perpetual inventory form and spot check it daily.

PROFIT THROUGH FOLLOWING RECIPES

Once you have decided on the markup of an item, check to make sure it is being made up as you costed it. How did you develop its selling price?

If you cost out a beef stew at $1.75 for 6 ozs. and you find you are putting out 7 ozs. for $1.75, this is a direct avenue for profit loss.

PROFIT THROUGH ASKING

Don't be ashamed to ask where a lower rate of interest can be obtained. Ask questions about your agreement with the attorney, insurance man, consultant. Ask questions, compare, then check.

Business mortgage rates depend on many things, mainly the individuals applying and their ability to pay back. Among many other considerations are the quality of the property, equipment, reputation of the business, and the degree of risks taken by the lending institution. These are all factors that determine the rate and cause it to fluctuate up or down. The larger the term of the loan, the higher the rate of interest charged.

The following is an example of the difference 2 percent points makes when borrowing money.

Let's assume you were buying a business or committing to a dollar expenditure of $75,000—having been accepted by a lending institution, you had a $45,000 mortgage (putting $30,000 as a down payment), your rate of interest being either 13 percent or 15 percent, the following will illustrate the same amount of borrowed dollars with a 2 percent differential.

Figure 1		Figure 2
75,000	Purchasing Cost	75,000
30,000	Down Payment	30,000
45,000	Amount owed	45,000

45,000 paid back in 15 years
pay back cost monthly:
$569.36 – principal and
          interest per
          month

45,000 paid back in 15 years
pay back cost monthly:
$629.82 – principal and
          interest per month

A saving of $60.46 per month or $725.52 per year. In terms of net profit, this $725.52 you saved represents approximately 10 percent of $7,000 worth of sales. Simply stated, you would have to sell approximately $7,000 worth of food, and if you operated efficiently enough to yield an approximate 10 percent net figure. Train yourself to think in these terms. Success in the food service industry is being able to adapt and achieve in every area of need.

PROFIT THROUGH COOKING PROPERLY

If you cook a roast and must rush its cooking process by increasing the temperature, you will have a greater degree of shrinkage in that piece of meat. If you allow it to cook at the proper temperature you will keep the quality of the meat and eliminate, or considerably decrease the shrinkage.

BUYING RETAIL

A restaurant operator considered himself a smart man but could not understand why the food cost was so high. He was not aware that the manager was, in emergencies, buying bread, rolls, hamburger and other items at retail prices. In order to cover poor purchasing methods the manager was not telling the owner of this practice, which remained undetected until the manager was out sick for a week. You must always buy wholesale and it is imperative for you to know what goes on at all times in your business regarding specials and promotions offered by salespeople. Delegating responsibility does not mean that you can be less vigilant about the costs and operation of your business.

CONTROL CHECK UNITY

Insist that one check be written for each customer. Write (or have a preprint made of each item on the menu,) on the check, every item served, so your number of meals sold per day can be checked to determine whether or not an item is profitable enough to stay on the menu. Check the waiters'/waitresses' checks for additions, subtractions and selling price of items. It may happen that they will serve a friend a club steak for $2.75 when it is priced at $3.75. If you fail to analyze the checks you may suffer more profit loss.

HAVE A SAFE

Invest in a good safe. Collect money from cash register several times daily, and deposit it in the safe which should be kept locked at all times during the day. Never leave money in the safe overnight. Get into the habit of making daily deposits. The safe should be located in an area where no customers, employees, salespeople, delivery people, etc. can see it.

PAYING BY CHECK

It is accepted practice in the restaurant business to pay by check, so that you have a record of whom you have paid. But there will be small pay outs that will be paid by cash. Use your daily food purchasing form (see Control Form Section) to keep track of these payments.

Find out if you are eligible for a 1 percent or 2 percent discount if bills are paid within a certain time. Discuss with your supplier the possibility of deducting 1-2 percent of the face of the invoice if you pay the bill within a certain period. Be sure you do not find you are paying *more* than the 1-2 percent discount because the supplier has given you the discount while raising the prices without your knowledge. Insist that if a company raises prices you must be informed first.

PROFIT/LOSS STATEMENT

It is wise to summarize your business as the attached Profit and Loss Statement shows. Doing this monthly is suggested, although

PROFIT AND LOSS STATEMENT

Date _____

Food Sales
Food Cost
Gross Profit
Salaries and Wages
Payroll Taxes and Benefits
                                            Total _____

Union Dues
Utilities
Telephone
Maintenance
Cleaning
Supplies
China-Glassware
Silverware
Paper Goods
Menus
Laundry
Uniforms
Petty Cash
Advertising
Credit Cards
                                            Total _____
Profit After Depreciation   _____
Rent   _____
Taxes, Licenses   _____
Interest   _____
Net Profit   _____

This form is a suggested one you may want to use monthly or weekly to recap each area listed. You may well find yourself adding sections.

it may be more work. You will then be able to know each month how your profit or loss stands. It means you must keep accurate monthly accounts of purchases, repairs, payroll, etc. The benefits received by doing it this way outweigh the disadvantages. By doing this monthly accounting you can match and compare the ratio of cost as it relates to sales, and if you find costs too high you can act immediately the same week to cut them for the next month. The secret is to keep a record of the exact monthly charges of the month in which the expenses occurred.

Other questions that will be answered by doing this are:

1. Is the inventory on hand too high?
2. Am I carrying stock that doesn't sell?
3. If so, what can I do about it?
4. Is the profit I'm making average, low or high?
5. How can I improve the profit picture without hurting the business?

SUMMARY: When a restaurant fails the manager or owner blames everything and everyone—the equipment, location, employees, bank, even the government, but never is it his/her fault. The truth is that many businesses fail because the owner/operator never took the time to study a book on the subject, had no knowledge of food preparation, was not able to communicate with people, had no business knowledge (knowledge in any business *is* power), did not understand what profit really is, did not stay abreast of the industry, and did not really watch the business. It is a cash business, and you will have a great deal of money in your possession all at one time. The biggest mistake most restaurant owners make is to believe that it is all their money, when in truth the money is there for paying bills. A person must learn *not* to spend money that is only entrusted to them. It is a false feeling that can easily be acquired if the constant flow of cash is not viewed in the proper perspective. Remember that!

Profit is one thing you cannot do without in any business. To make a profit you must always be on the alert by watching every angle of your business; how the food is prepared, how it is stored, the employees' attitudes, their work habits plus customer acceptance. Many things could be listed that would help you make a profit. Learn to observe each situation and think it out, then ask yourself, "How does this affect the profit?" You will be successful if you challenge and train yourself to be profit conscious. Profit is the only thing that will enable you to expand, to give raises to employees and to yourself. Most of all it is needed to make your business survive and grow.

Have a plan of work, and work your plan. New ventures always experience some growing pains, but as employees get accustomed to doing things as you want them done, and when you want them done, the work will be easier, and everyone, including yourself, will find the working day going more smoothly as time goes on.

As everyone becomes more proficient in doing their respective jobs they will become more efficient and self-assured and this will become apparent to the customers in the way they are served, and in the quality of the food.   This will also help improve the profit picture.

QUESTIONS

1. How much must a business gross for the owner to earn $15,000.00 a year?

2. What are three ways to produce a better profit?

3. The owner/manager should know the daily cost of the rent.   What other daily costs should be known?

4. What factors will help produce a profit?

5. Why should only a week's supply of inventory be kept on hand?

6. Why is it important to make up an item the same each and every time?

7. Why is it important to keep a monthly Profit and Loss Statement?

10
Today's
Management Techniques

It is important that the owner/operator understand what a self-actualized person is. It is someone who has learned how to understand the feelings, of others, happy *and* miserable, and who has learned the importance of motivation. A mentally healthy person accepts themselves and others easily.

The growth of any business is dependent upon the quality of management. In business today one must master the science of management. The days of "take it or leave it" are gone. By taking a good management course you can learn those things which will help make you a qualified owner/operator able to handle people.

When any owner/operator stops learning he/she is finished. The average person going into management today may possibly return to college for a year of full-time study twice during their career. Their training will also include separate seminars, short courses, and it will be reinforced by reading the many educational and business publications available.

PLEASING THE CUSTOMER

We all know when business is slow, most restaurants give good service. What develops a good reputation is your business giving good service even when you are short of help, the equipment breaks down, you don't receive a delivery, etc. This is when it's important to give deluxe service. How many times have you heard someone say "Let's leave. We'll never get waited on. They're too busy and they're short of help."

INDIVIDUAL BUSINESS

Many restaurants can't be sold easily because the original developer of the restaurant created such an individual tie to the business that it is next to impossible to get someone else to take it over. I know of one restaurant man who wanted to sell his business, which was very successful, but could not do so. The reason was he did all the cooking, worked the pantry area, spoke to 95 percent of the customers on a first name basis, worked approximately 100 hours a week and did all the baking of pies and cakes. This business was so demanding that without his work out-put and presence, the same quality of consistency that had taken him forty years to develop, could not be matched by any of the potential buyers of the business and they realized this.

OWNER'S BUSINESS LIFE INSURANCE

An owner/operator should carefully consider additional life insurance when buying a business. What would happen if he/she died? The time to plan for this is when the business is purchased. Ask yourself these questions:

1. How can I protect my business in the event of my death if my family is not interested in running it?
2. How will the money I owe be paid?
3. How will my family live?
4. What are the complications involved in taking in a partner?
5. How does it affect my family taxwise if the business is all paid for and worth a lot of money?
6. What happens if my key employees quit in case of my death?

GOOD MANAGEMENT HABITS

To manage people, you've got to manage yourself first. Let us discuss you, the owner/operator of a business, and consider how you rate yourself.

Your personal standard of conduct as it relates to your business, thinking and life must be above reproach at all times. Your employees will be watching your every move. Your reactions to various situations will be evaluated by them. In their private and social lives you and your business will be discussed by them, so your actions, talk and decisions must reflect good moral and ethical traits. Remember that the disgruntled employee who leaves your employ will take along an impression of you and your business. Strive for fair play, equal rights and benefits, always expect high standards and set a good example.

Set up your company policies and expect your employees to abide by them. If you expect them to remember, you must also. For example, if you are supposed to open at 7:00 a.m. and your employees are waiting at the door for you at 7:15 a.m. you are not setting policy, you are creating problems.

A good owner/operator learns early to be *firm, fair* and to *follow through*. Spell out your orders—be clear, be certain they are understood and make it a habit to check back to see that they are being carried out correctly. The employee needs to know you have checked and appreciates your comments on the way the orders were carried out.

TRAINING AND DEALING WITH EMPLOYEES

The restaurant business is a people business and the way you deal with these people could determine your success. Remember the golden rule in dealing with all people you come in contact with. Let your staff feel they are a part of what is going on. Be interested in *all* people. Praise your staff in front of other staff members. Make sure you ask for their opinions, suggestions and problems. Give them a feeling of security but be firm and fair. Don't play favorites. Be sure to check and comment on their performance. When you find problems in the restaurant, follow them through all the way, find out how they can be eliminated and kept from happening again.

Train your help to do other jobs than their own, so if someone is sick, busy or on vacation you will have replacements.

New employees are costly to train unless you have an outline of what you want accomplished. In hiring new people, consider the following points:

    1. Can the applicant take the pace of walking and standing?

2. What is his/her general health? (If he/she isn't well, he/she cannot work well)
3. Does the applicant have experience? What kind was it? Why did he/she leave? Is his/her past experience able to be substantiated?
4. Does he/she seem able to follow orders, directions? What if he/she disagrees with the directions?
5. Is he/she able to handle the work schedule? (i.e. can he/she work weekends, nights, etc.?)
6. Does he/she give the impression that he/she enjoys working in a "people situation"?

Mismatched Applicant

You may hire a person who seems well qualified. They have told you they have had all kinds of experience but when they are hired and have been given a fair probation period in which to do the work they simply cannot do it. Do you and your business a favor. If you feel they have a good potential for the business send them to a school for training. If you feel they will never be able to master the job call them in and terminate them, after explaining your reasons. Don't just close your eyes to problems that will not improve.

APPLICATION FOR EMPLOYMENT

Purchase any type of job application form from a good stationery store. Each prospective employee should be instructed to fill it out in detail. Be sure the application includes a place for references, and ask applicant's permission to check any reference listed. As you check each reference ask that person for suggestions on anyone else you can contact to help you make a fair decision about the applicant. Be fair. Remember you were once in the prospective employee's position!

INTERVIEWING PROSPECTIVE NEW EMPLOYEES

Put the person at ease. Learn as much as possible about his/her life style, home, family, likes, dislikes, etc. while you have him/her there. Choose questions from the application form for more detailed information such as where and for whom the applicant has previously worked, what kind of work was required, etc. Explain the job opening in detail, the benefits and the disadvantages. Be honest, tell it like it is. Once you have checked all references and evaluated the applicant's qualifications in relation to the job they are applying for, then you can make your decision to hire (or not) and the amount of training that will be necessary. Make note of all special skills this person may have; baker, chef, etc. Note his/her attitude, ability to get along with others, flexibility in doing it your way instead of the way he/she was accustomed to doing it previously, and whether or not he/she would be resistant to change.

PAY SCALE

Start your employees off at a fair wage, based on what you can afford, their experience, and your need at the time. Also consider what other restaurants in your area are paying their employees. You really do get what you pay for, so don't build a reputation for giving inadequate pay or poor increases.

EMPLOYEES' LIMITATIONS

Realize that certain people are suited for certain levels of work. Do not try to overmatch a person in a position right at the start. Do not expect too much. Praise for accomplishments and correct when needed. Remember that courtesy is essential. A person washing dishes does not like to be called a "pot or pan" person or dishwasher. Refer to the dishwasher as a "sanitation" person or attendant.

HIRING RELATIVES

Before hiring relatives be certain they will work and expect to be treated just as any other employee. Failure to make this clear could result in harmful undertones and hurt business.

ORIENTATION FOR NEW EMPLOYEES

Following is a list of things the new worker should be informed about:

1. Spell out exactly what the job is and ask if there are any questions.
2. Introduce the new worker to the person who will be their boss.
3. Explain pay scale and whether or not they are to be paid by cash or check, and what day is payday. Explain the benefits (hospital insurance for example).
4. Explain how overtime will be worked if there is any.
5. Let them know how you handle employees' suggestions and complaints. (An employee suggestion box is a good morale booster.)
6. Tell them who they are to call if they are sick.
7. Inform them about uniforms. Who pays for them and how many will be issued.
8. Explain your policy on smoking, breaks, lunch, tips, etc.
9. Invite any other questions.

Remember *your* first day on a new job!

DRESSING FOR WORK

If you, the owner/manager are neat and correctly dressed, you will set a good example for your employees. If you feel good and are dressed neatly, you will usually work better. The same is true for employees, which makes for a smooth, efficient business.

For Men Employees:

1. Wear a regulation coat or apron and hat.
2. A clean shirt, shined shoes and pressed pants show they have pride in their appearance and in their job.
3. A clean-shaven face and neatly trimmed hair are a must.
4. Wear I.D. badge.

For Women Employees:

1. Regulation uniform as required.
2. Aprons with neatly tied bows.
3. Head bands or hair nets.

4. Hosiery.
5. A simple hair-do, clean fingernails and little jewelry.

Daily baths and use of a deodorant is a must for *all* employees. Hair nets or hats are required by law. Closed shoes—not sneakers—are safer than sandals.

RULES FOR EMPLOYEES (post in conspicuous place)

1. Do not chew gum.
2. Do not smoke while on duty.
3. Don't loiter in kitchen or halls. Your job is to service customers.
4. Do not leave clothes, handbags or personal items near registers. A place should be assigned for them.
5. No loud talking or horseplay even in areas behind the scenes.
6. Don't allow full ash trays to remain on tables especially during the meal.
7. Don't hand silverware, cups, etc. to customers improperly.
8. Don't allow food or beverages to be given away.
9. Don't scratch head, chew nails, etc.
10. Don't argue with fellow employees.
11. Don't lean on equipment, tables, counters.
12. Don't eat in customer area. (The owner/operator should assign an eating area in kitchen or at a specific table in the dining room for the staff.)
13. Don't take part in telling or in spreading rumors.
14. Don't let your private life interfere with the job you were hired to do.
15. Watch for swinging door going into kitchen.
16. Check floors and tables for items spilled. Keep them clean and safe.
17. Don't overload trays.
18. Be careful in handling sharp items.
19. Handle dishes quietly.
20. Tell customers if plates are hot.
21. If you break a glass or dish clean it up right away.
22. Work fast but do not rush. This causes accidents.
23. Waiter/waitress to stay in the area they are responsible for.

Safety in the Kitchen

1. Use cooking mitts in handling pots and pans.
2. Use the proper tools (don't use a knife as a screwdriver).
3. Everyone should know where the fire extinguisher is, and know how to use it. Explain the emergency lighting system in the same manner.
4. Before cleaning equipment make sure it has been turned off.
5. Use a dry cutting board for slicing and cutting.
6. Put all cleaning items away (don't leave mops and buckets where they can be tripped over).
7. Employees should wear sensible shoes—no sandals or sneakers. There is always a danger of hot things splashing or sharp, heavy objects falling.

TRAINING PLAN

1. Do you have a well-planned training program?

2. Do you give complete instructions for the performance of all the work involved in all jobs?

3. Do you encourage employees to take advantage of opportunities available in the community for additional vocational training such as attending a culinary school or a related subject school?

4. Only certain employees should operate the cash register. Delegate this to those who are quick, accurate and good at figures. They should know how to check for counterfeit money, how to handle money orders and traveler's checks and what approach to use when dealing with short-change artists.

5. All employees dealing with customers should be neat, alert to customer's wants, gracious and patient, especially when handling complaints.

6. If an employer expects loyalty and cooperation from employees he/she must be fair, thoughtful and pleasant to all employees at all times.

7. Employees waiting on table should know what each dish and bowl is used for, how to set a table properly and what side work is involved in their job.

8. Employees should be instructed in the correct way to approach a customer, how to take an order and the right time to make other food suggestions.

9. Knowing how to place an order with the chef or cook and the correct way to place food on the table helps employees do a better job.

10. Employees are expected to be cheerful and pleasant in their contacts with customers but excessive familiarity or the showing of partiality to friends should not be permitted.

11. The rule concerning tips in your establishment should be understood by employees *before* they wait on their first table.

12. Liquor service is a specialized service and should only be undertaken by those having had proper training and instruction.

Never be satisfied with average service. Expect 100 percent from employees in performance, give customers 100 percent in food and service, and you yourself must give 100 percent in effort, time, material and money.

View your business critically. Check things that need taking care of (dirty windows, rest rooms, etc.) and have the work done.

When an employee does something wrong, correct it at once in a professional manner. A big mistake is to look the other way or postpone correcting the situation. This is poor management and will be reflected in your business image.

Bring these things out during your training sessions and get everyone to participate in the discussions.

Ways to Train New Employees

1. First you must know how to do the job yourself.
2. Put the trainee at ease. Some general small talk is helpful before you begin.
3. Have the complete job breakdown before you. Explain it step by step. An example of a job breakdown can be as follows:

GRILL OPERATOR

a. Place all orders to the left of the pick-up sheet.

b. Prepare orders from checks on a left to right basis.

c. Wipe knife dry after each sandwich is cut.

d. Use paprika and parsley on all dinners.

    e. Strain all vegetables prior to serving.

    f. Turn on call system when orders are ready.

    g. Coordinate frying items, baking items, grilling items simultaneously.   Observe and control your entire sector of preparation.

4. Get them interested in the job.

5. Actually demonstrate the job.   Do it yourself or put them with someone who you know will train them to do the job exactly as you want it done.

6. Demonstrate and talk the person through the operation.

7. Explain why the job is important.

8. Stress the key points.

9. Instruct clearly and patiently.   Remember that what is simple to you now is very confusing and scary to a new person.

10. Answer any questions the trainee may have.

11. Now try them out on the job.

12. Have trainee explain job to you or to the person working with them.

13. Give them a 3″ x 5″ pad and encourage them to write down any questions they may have.

14. Correct trainees on errors as they are made.

15. Continue and repeat the operation until you feel that they understand and are comfortable doing it.

16. Follow through.   Check on performance, encourage questions, tactfully point out mistakes and evaluate truthfully when you tell them how they made out.

Motivation for Employers and Employees

One of the hardest things to do is to openly admit that you don't know how to do something.   Remember this when you train people. Tell them you have felt this way and know the feeling.

How do you get people motivated?

1. Make people feel independent and self sufficient by trusting them to do things the way you want them done.

2. Give your employees a feeling of adequacy and self respect.

3. Most people are not properly trained in the food service business because management doesn't train properly.

Management dictates and lectures but doesn't train by example and doesn't listen to employees. Listen to them!

EMPLOYEE APPRAISAL

It is wise to evaluate your employees on a regular basis for wage increases. If you feel the employee doesn't merit an increase you should sit with them and openly discuss the reasons. Keep a sheet on each employee and once a week jot down any good or bad points that employee showed in that week. In this manner you will develop a pattern to help you reach a decision; to increase employee's salary or keep it as it is. Today all successful owners and managers periodically review their help before giving wage increases.

Keep a log on each employee that includes the number of times you had to correct for mistakes, lateness, rudeness, laziness, attitude, etc. When you evaluate your employees mention these things to them. It is also helpful, should you need to terminate an employee, to have the log to refer to for substantiation of your decision.

HOW DO YOUR EMPLOYEES SEE YOU?

1. How good is your judgment?
2. Are you good at setting up things?
3. Can you work and be a good leader at the same time?
4. Can you hire or fire employees with self-confidence?
5. Can you overcome discouragement?
6. Do you have a temper that you take out on others?
7. Do you use coarse language?
8. Are you a worrier?
9. Are you sincere?

Most employees want to work for an appreciative, fair owner/ operator who sets reasonable standards, is someone they can respect and whom they can trust to reward their efforts. How do you rate yourself from the list of management traits below?

A manager should (1) relate well with all people and mangement personnel; (2) portray an air of confidence, a take-charge, confident attitude, not one of crisis or panic; (3) be able to keep composure under all circumstances; (4) seek methods to promote more productivity among the help, and methods to reduce operating costs which are in the owner/operator's area of responsibility; (5) is not be a "nine to five" person—must be willing to give as much time as necessary for the success of the business; (6) work the hours the business calls for, especially at holiday times; (7) always be aware of sales and figures, and be aware of how the restaurant is doing now, how it did last week, last month, last year; (8) talk with customers; (9) lead by setting a good example; (10) always be ready to develop product knowledge; (11) be a good listener and keep an open mind; (12) not take criticism personally, but use it to broaden business knowledge and to expand the business; (13) get involved in and be aware of every aspect of the business; (14) always be prepared to write down customer information, reminders or suggestions on a pad carried in a pocket or attached to a clipboard; and (15) always remember, either by what is written on a pad or by some other method, to follow through and do the important things that require follow up, checking on, or supervision, and *never* use the old cliche, "I forgot."

The above are true management traits that can be worked on and eventually become part of your makeup that will stay with you forever . . .

DELEGATING WORK RESPONSIBILITY

Some owners want to do everything themselves, but remember, you have a paid staff.

Look for people with the three I's—initiative, interest and imagination. The person in charge must have drive, be strong-willed and he/she should have enough ego to want to look good, but not to the point of antagonizing others.

OPENING THE RESTAURANT

1. Who will turn on the grills?
2. List items needed for the sandwich board. One person assigned to check it every day.
3. List all kitchen needs. One person must check them and make a list of items to be ordered.

4. Someone must check china, cutlery, etc. before customers arrive.
5. Who is to be in charge of the safe? Are there enough singles and change as a back up or will someone have to go to the bank?

BEING A PART OF THE TEAM

Each member of your staff should feel as though they are part of a team. Teamwork is instilled through an open attitude, cooperation, interest, motivation and the knowledge that each individual's efforts are important to the ultimate goal, which is good business and a net profit.

THE RUSH HOUR

1. Every food service operation is faced with a period when it is filled to capacity (rush hour times). This is when many businesses develop a reputation for giving excellent, good, fair or poor service.

2. Every phase of work in the operation should be scheduled for this time and ready for it.

3. These hours will soon form a pattern and can be anticipated before they happen.

EFFECT OF WORKING CONDITIONS

The hours prior to a meal are always busy ones in the production or setting up part of a restaurant. The food being handled requires lifting cases, opening cans and other strenuous work. Even if all the facilities are good (new equipment, good light, air, etc.) the workers are still exposed to high temperatures for a long period of time. They are also confined to a small area to accomplish this work in. This type of working condition is fatiguing. This is mentioned to make you aware of what happens when a cook or baker working under these conditions suddenly gets an excessive number of orders to fill. It will very likely cause them to be irritable.

CUSTOMER BUILDERS

1. Have employees check glasses, silverware, napkins, dishes each time they set up (before customers arrive) looking for spots, chips, bent or dirty items.

2. Train employees to set up each place with all utensils, napkins and glasses of water placed properly prior to taking the order.

3. Number each booth and stool. Have waiter/waitress write the number and their name on each check.

4. Train your people to suggest premeal cocktails, soups, specials, sandwiches, desserts, etc.

5. Train waiter/waitress to take order correctly getting the details customer requests such as "no gravy," "two vegetables," etc.

6. Train them to give orders to the cook correctly. Have a system for trying to salvage errors such as when the wrong salad dressing is used, etc.

7. Have a system to let waiters/waitresses know when their orders are ready.

8. Train them to examine the checks before they pick up their orders so they will get the right one.

9. Make sure they pick orders up promptly as hot food must be served hot and cold food served cold.

10. If an order is made up incorrectly have them return it to the kitchen for correction.

11. Make sure condiments are within reach of customers.

12. Train waiters/waitresses to carry food properly. It should be at a comfortable height for them but carried in a way to show it off to tables they pass.

13. Handle complaints tactfully.

14. Wipe up spilled foods and liquids at once.

15. Remove dishes as soon as customer finishes but do not create the feeling that they are being rushed.

16. Make sure all meals, drinks and desserts are prepared the same way each time.

17. Keep a menu with the correct prices listed near the preparation area and have waiters/waitresses check their tabs for errors before handing them to customers.

18. Replace napkins, silverware, etc. at once if they are dropped by the customer during the meal.

CLEAN-UP TIME

1. Set the example by always doing your part.
2. Handle dishes, glassware and silverware quietly.
3. In bus tray or in dishwashing area separate the glassware, plates and silverware for clean up. Have a separate section for garbage disposal.
4. Establish a cleaning schedule for small and large equipment.
5. Make sure large containers are emptied into smaller ones when contents get low and that all containers, jars, etc. are properly covered.
6. Make sure leftovers such as butter, milk, rolls, etc. are not thrown out but are salvaged and stored properly if not used.
7. Utensils, pots, trays, etc. should be carefully dried and put in their specific locations.

SAVING STEPS

1. Teach employees to coordinate their efforts.
2. They should be trained to replenish any item they may run out of during serving time *before* it is completely used up. If they are busy someone else should be asked to do this.
3. Carefully observe all operations looking for ways to make things easier and to cut down on unnecessary walking.
4. One person might have to be given charge of the dessert/beverage area or the salad set-up area during busy periods to cut down on walking.
5. During busy periods it might be wise to put out extra supplies such as spoons, trays, plates, etc. and to position them for easy access for the staff.
6. Look for the new equipment, the trends in business methods and foods that can cut down on walking now being done.

A WELL-MANAGED RESTAURANT

A well-managed restaurant makes every customer feel welcome. "How are you today, Mr. Jones?" The individual attention may be just the thing to bring him back as a steady customer. He will be impressed by the fact that no matter how busy you are you still have time to smile and greet him pleasantly. This good habit will also rub off on your employees. It is not necessary to be over friendly but if done in moderation it is in good taste, and demonstrates good showmanship on a business level.

HOW TO BE DIPLOMATIC

Let us assume that you are called on to settle an argument by a customer you know well. You must be fair, truthful and diplomatic. It is sad but true that if you win an argument with a customer you may lose that customer's business. Although customers can be wrong, employees must understand that since their jobs depend on customers the customer is "King."

By following the steps set down for training employees you will be able to match the employees to the jobs you want them to do. Training, correction, follow-through and periodic evaluation eliminates the possibility of the employees setting their own standards of work performance, cuts down on hiring new personnel (a time-consuming task) and results in fewer terminations.

SALES TECHNIQUES AND GREETINGS

"May I serve you, sir (madame or miss)?" is an excellent greeting. If you know the person's last name use it. Be friendly but business-like at all times. Instruct your employees to make suggestions: When a sandwich is ordered have them ask, "Would you like a side order of french fries?" and when apple pie is ordered have them suggest a scoop of ice cream, etc. These helpful suggestions can increase the check average.

OWNER'S RULES

1. Don't expect miracles. Be patient.
2. Be sincere, honest and fair with all people.
3. Don't consider your staff as a tool. They are people with feelings, emotions and private lives who must work for their basic needs (food, shelter, clothes).

4. Don't let *your* private life affect the way you conduct your business or the way you treat your staff.

GUEST CHECKS VERSUS REGISTER READINGS

Pick up all guest checks personally on a daily basis and add them up to give you a total dollar figure. Check the figure against the register reading. The two figures should be the same. If they are not find out why.

TAKEOUT RESTAURANT BUSINESS

This is a part of the business that is very profitable because the customer is not using your restaurant to eat in. This is a saving as the customer does not use table, counter or booth space. Customer turnover is much greater in the takeout end of your business. With these thoughts in mind develop a speedy takeout business. Be sure you have the proper supplies for takeout service. Do not use improper fitting lids, poor quality bags, etc. The secret of a successful takeout business is fast service and good food. The takeout food should be the same, both in appearance and quality, at the place it's being consumed as if it were being served in the restaurant.

Takeout business is very profitable. Develop it.

WHAT IS THE IMAGE OF YOUR RESTAURANT?

Have you taken the time to check your operation as you would if you were a customer or as you would check if you were eating in a competitor's restaurant? What would you look for? Here are some things that people expect to find:

1. A clean restaurant at all times.
2. Good food prepared the same every time.
3. Good service from polite and well-trained employees.
4. Pleasant surroundings.
5. Capable managers who understand and like people and are fair in dealing with customers and employees.
6. Value.

Loitering

To allow loitering only asks for trouble. Discourage it. Do not take it upon yourself to get rid of those people that hang around your establishment if such an occasion arises. Get friendly with the police department. Let them know you want to run a good, respectable business. Never take matters into your own hands but work with the police.

ADVERTISING YOUR BUSINESS

You will need some form of advertising although the best kind is by word of mouth. Some of the more common methods of advertising are as follows:

Television

This is quite expensive for a small business person but if you can afford it the effectiveness of the exposure is worth the cost.

Yellow Pages

These listings in the phone book get results even if you have been in the same place of business for a lifetime. It is of help to tourists who do not know restaurants in the area. Costs are usually based on page space.

Radio

This has always been an effective way to get a message to the people. The cost is based on the amount of time used and the time of day. Trade-off plans are sometimes used whereby the radio cost is paid by the restaurant operator in meals to radio station operators, guests or by a tie-in promotion.

Newspaper

The newspaper cost is by inches, position, type of coverage, etc. It also depends on whether or not it will be daily, weekly, etc. This is still a good method to use.

Buses, Transit Cars

Rates are less than for other types of advertising. As a rule it is very effective as the public gets the message every time they use this type of transportation.

Billboards

The space is rented. Usually the cost is based on the billboard and the length of time the sign stays up.

Reviews

A food editor or a restaurant critic can be called to come in unannounced and will make an honest evaluation of the restaurant. Then an article is written on the findings. This exposure can be the start of your business success if the critic was well satisfied. Be advised that they will print what they experience.

Your Own Promotions

This can be done by table tents, pass out menus, match books, postcards, place mats, special of the month tied in with the time of year, special buttons worn by employees. These are all ways you can promote your business along with methods already suggested. As you travel look for what others in the restaurant business are doing to advertise. Would any of their ideas work for you?

Service Reports

You can obtain various reports that will tell you the present market cost of meat, vegetables, dairy products, etc. These reports are good if your operation merits the cost of a subscription. It is an excellent tool to know and understand the market on a daily basis. Your local library can help you.

Special Reports

Your library and the Small Business Administration office are excellent sources to tell you where to obtain various reports as relate to what percentage of profit you should be making for your type of business and also the direct percentage of the actual category itself. For example: what your food cost, payroll, rent, etc. should be on an average. Some of the reports available to you are:

1. Dunn and Bradstreet
2. Robert Morris Associates
3. Accounting Corporation of America
4. National Cash Register (Retail expenses)

Check List of Things You Must Consider

1. Bank Deposit Procedure.
2. Payroll Procedure.
3. Bank Americard.
4. Store Opening Procedure.
5. Store Closing Procedure.
6. Safe Combination.
7. Register. How to close it, change tape, etc.
8. Forms to close out register.
9. Beat last year's book. Daily sales entry.
10. Light switches marked separately from refrigerator and freezer switches.
11. All door opeining and closing procedures.
12. Refund procedure.
13. Back up money.

OWNER'S-MANAGER RESPONSIBILITIES

Before the rush starts check every area—the grills, kitchen, parking lot, dining room, etc. to make sure everything is ready to go. If it is not tell someone what needs to be done to get it ready and then check to make sure it was taken care of.

When the rush does come all of your people should be ready to do nothing but take care of the customers. Your cook should make sure how the food is being served and should correct anything that is wrong. The owner/operator is the coordinator who keeps the operation going smoothly. Some of the things the owner/manager should do are (1) Make sure checks are written clearly so cashier can check and know whether or not customer is being charged correct price; (2) watch to see if waiters/waitresses are pleasant and are suggesting additional items to help increase sales; (3) go to every area and make sure all are okay; (4) help physically in any area when needed but do not stay in any one place; (5) deliver plates to waiters/ waitresses when they are ready; (6) Shuffle help to any area where it is needed just until work is caught up. The owner/manager must be "Johnny on the Spot" to keep it all running smoothly.

TO BE A BETTER OWNER/OPERATOR

One method of learning how to be a better owner/operator and develop management skills is to study the reasons for the failure of some restaurants. Don't become vulnerable to the same pitfalls yourself.

Remember also that as sole owner/operator you will play many different roles.

One particular example comes to my mind. I once knew a very capable chef who worked in a highly successful restaurant. He had a very pleasing personality and liked people. One day he told me he had been working in the same restaurant for almost 30 years and felt he had made the restaurant what it was and had absolutely nothing to show for it. He had given his notice and shortly opened his own restaurant. In a fairly short time this man lost thousands of dollars, his wife left him and he ended up as a chef's helper at the same restaurant where he had been the chef.

The lesson to be learned here is that our friend did not realize that his input as chef was only a part of the larger picture. The efforts and contributions of many others along with his efforts made the restaurant a success. He lacked a knowledge of recordkeeping. Although he bought the finest food and supplies he did not know (and did not take the time to learn) how to control his inventory. He could plan his kitchen well but could not plan other departments of the business. He lacked much needed expertise in marketing and could not assume all the roles necessary to make it on his own.

Our chef friend soon learned that although he had people whom he paid to take care of bookkeeping functions, he lacked knowledge in the following areas:

How to purchase all goods.

How to determine a selling price.

How to budget, advertise, etc. which are the responsibility of management.

Never assume that one skill is enough to make you successful in this business. It is a combination of many ingredients and learned skills.

Many owner/operators have risen straight through their level of competency and not replenished their information on how to stay up with the times.

The food service industry is constantly changing in many ways so you must expand your knowledge. By going to seminars, workshops, taking courses and relating to other people with an open mind you will be developing a success base.

IMPORTANT DATES TO REMEMBER

Holidays are very important to the owner/operator for the following reasons:

1. Your business may be greatly increased or you may be closed.
2. If you open you will have to make plans to order more goods, increase the staff, possibly put out a special menu or decorate to coincide with the time of year.
3. If your business is closed that holiday you must make plans to store foods properly and plan food so that the left-over factor doesn't carry over to the holiday.

The following list of important dates will help in planning the measures you must take in adjusting the many aspects of your business for the day.

New Year's Day
Lincoln's Birthday
Valentine's Day
Washington's Birthday (observed)
Washington's Birthday
Ash Wednesday
St. Patrick's Day
Census Day
Palm Sunday

Good Friday
Easter Sunday
Passover
Mother's Day
Armed Forces Day
Victoria Day (Canada)
Memorial Day (observed)
Memorial Day
Flag Day
Father's Day
Dominion Day (Canada)
Independence Day
Labor Day
Rosh Hashanah
Yom Kippur
Thanksgiving Day (Canada)
Columbus Day (observed)
Columbus Day
Halloween
Election Day
Veterans Day
Thanksgiving Day
Hanukkah
Christmas Day

SUMMARY: Efficient, well-trained and pleasant personnel are an asset in any business. In the restaurant business where employees are dealing with the public, they are not only an asset but a vital link between the customer and the owner/operator. Their professionalism in serving, their attitude toward customers and the relationships between employees and the person operating the business can well be deciding factors in whether or not this will be a successful operation.

The owner/operator must (1) make sure all personnel hired are neat, personable and able to do the job for which they were hired; (2) train employees to perform their duties to the specifications that were spelled out before they were hired; (3) watch closely for anything that can be corrected or changed to make an employee's work more efficient and easier; (4) check to make sure work load is evenly divided; and (5) treat *all* employees alike. Be fair, firm and courteous. Show no favoritism.

As the owner/manager of a business, ask yourself this "Would I work and make money for my type of person?" Remember that when you are dealing with employees, customers, sales people, bankers, lawyers, etc. you are either making a good or bad impression. They all can (and most likely will) spread good or bad reports regarding your ability to manage the people who work for you.

Have a set pattern of what you want done. Some food service operators do very little planning when it comes to training their own people. Everything is a "hit or miss" type of operation.

QUESTIONS

1. A good manager learns early to be ___ , ___ and to ___ .

2. When giving an order, a manager must be ___ , ___ and make it a habit to ___ .

3. List five of the things that must be done in training new employees.

4. Name three things that create a good business image.

5. Why should an appraisal sheet be kept on each employee?

6. List three items that should be included on an application for employment.

7. What are some of the traits a manager should have?

8. Give two reasons why a cook or baker might become irritable.

9. What should the owner/operator do to prevent employees from becoming irritable.?

11
Service Professionalism

Service is a very important ingredient. Customers expect profession-alism in uniforms, servicing of food, and liquor, a reasonable noise level, adequate heat, lighting, and ventilation, plates, packing methods, etc. All these factors, if properly organized, prove to the customers that they are getting professional service. These things will label you either as a pro or as an amateur in today's market.

The owner/operator must make sure that the people serving the customers observe the following procedures.

1. Have tables and seats wiped clean before the customer is seated. Keep an eagle eye out to see which customer sits down first. The rule is first come, first served. Give a pleasant smile and greeting to all. Once customer is seated promptly present them with the menu and a glass of water. After giving them time to make their selection, approach and say "May I take your order, please?"

If other customers are waiting let them know they have been noticed. A simple "I'll be with you in a moment" is all it takes.

What we have said so far:

a. We have a clean place to serve in.

b. A pleasant smile and greeting.

c. Menu and water.

Make sure each check is made out with the number of the table, booth or seat. Once this is done they will never have to ask "Who's the roast beef?" or "Who's the veal steak?" Some people might re-sent being called a roast beef or a veal steak.

Remove food from the left, beverages from the right. Use left hand when working to the left of a table and right hand when working from the right. Never reach in front of a customer to serve or remove an order.

2. *Taking the order.* Before taking an order have them check on the following things.

    a. Do they know all the prices on the menu?

    b. Do they know all the items on the menu so they can answer questions?

    c. Do they know something about the make-up of each plate?

All these things will help them to take a better order from the customer.

Have them make out a check for each customer served. Have item written on the check before serving the order. When they get busy and serve an item without writing in on the check, the customer is not charged for that item and this is a serious avenue of loss of profit.

Have them listen carefully to details: "no mayonnaise," "no pickle," "on rye." Orders made incorrectly not only result in "Profit Loss" but also result in customer dissatisfaction.

They should try to complete the order at one time and should try to suggest different items to the customer.

They should repeat the order back to the customer to be sure it is correct.

If there are any strange requests or items they do not understand, they should find out from the manager or owner and tell the customer as soon as possible.

3. *Placing the order.* Be sure whatever system used works with duplicate slips, spindle, hanging checks, microphones. One important thing for them to remember is to make sure they put in the order and, once it is in, to keep checking to see that someone else doesn't serve it by mistake.

4. *Most important.*

    a. To check all dishes, silverware, glasses to be sure they are not chipped, bent or spotted.

    b. To make certain the customer has water, napkin, and necessary silverware before serving the order.

    c. Pick up order as soon as it is ready.

d. Return for remake any food made incorrectly and tell the kitchen what is wrong. Let the customer know approximately how long it will take to correct.

e. To place dishes, silverware, and glassware as follows:

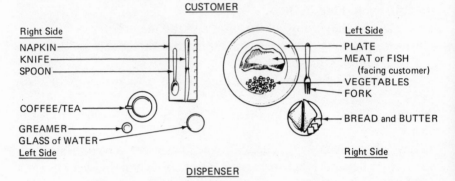

f. Move salt, pepper, sugar and other condiments close to the customer.

g. Refill water glasses when necessary.

h. When food or liquid is spilled wipe it up and replace it at once if necessary.

i. Make a replacement or substitution if the customer complains.

j. If customer doesn't ask for dessert suggest something tasty from the menu.

k. Remove dishes as soon as the customer is finished, but be sure they are finished. Never give a customer the feeling he/she is being rushed by snatching away the plate before he/she is finished.

5. *Collecting for the order.* Many restaurants do a poor job in presenting the check. Know when the customer is ready for it and check the figures before presenting it to them. Many mistakes are made when check totaling is rushed because a customer is waiting.

Never accuse a customer of trying to walk out without paying. If you see that it may happen present check and say "I'll take care of it for you," or "Please pay the cashier."

Another tip: If three guests come in together and ask for separate checks write the number three on back of each check so the cashier will know the group had three people together with three separate checks. This should be done for any number of people from two on up. If this is done and a customer drops a check or one gets destroyed accidentally, the cashier will know enough to say "I believe you had three people in this group. I only have two checks. Did someone drop one?"

    6. *Cleaning Up*. Those cleaning up should:

      a. Be sure to *place* dishes and silverware in boxes rather than throwing them.

      b. Use clean towels, cloths (fold into eighths or quarters) or sponges.

      c. Always wipe towards themselves.

      d. Wash out towels, cloths or sponges often.

      e. View work area with a critical eye. Do not be satisfied with average cleanliness. Always strive for perfection.

SUGGESTIVE SELLING

Anyone can take a written order, but a restaurant that has its people suggest additional items in a pleasant manner not only increases sales but satisfies the customer. Here are a few suggestions:

Customer asks for following:	Good restaurant people say:
Apple Pie	"With vanilla ice cream?"
Tuna Fish Sandwich	"Would you like French Fries or potato salad?"
Hamburger	"Would you like tomatoes on that?"

    The thinking is to build up the check average but also to get the customer to combine foods. In this way the customer will, in the future, order foods by combination and better their eating habits, as well as increase sales at the same time, so everyone gains.

CONSTANT FOLLOW-UP AND SUPERVISION

The food service industry has been labeled as having low employee productivity, and the biggest problem is that not many managers or owners train or supervise their employees enough. The specialists, trained chefs and bakers, are in the back of the house. The managers or owners are usually in their office or talking to salespeople or customers and no one is training on the spot, supervising on the spot and following up on the spot. Therefore the employees seek their own level as to standards of cleanliness, service and professionalism.

SUMMARY: A restaurant's good food, good location and good financing can easily be tarnished if it gets the reputation for poor service. Good service must start with the owner, manager and people in charge. You must teach employees what is to be done and exactly how it is to be done. Then comes constant follow-up to ensure it's being done properly. Any on-the-spot correction must be done in such a manner that employees realize you expect professionalism in servicing customers. In order to attain this the employee must be properly trained *in the beginning.* A big mistake many restaurants make is in having other employees train new people when they themselves have never been properly trained.

Service is a major offering of your business in today's market. It cannot be less than the best in town offered by pleasant, interested, neatly and cleanly dressed people.

QUESTIONS

1. What is service professionalism?

2. What steps should you follow in taking an order?

3. What is suggestive selling?

4. What should be done after the order is taken?

5. You should wait until customer asks for check before totaling it.
    True _____   False _____

6. It has been said that the food service industry has low employee productivity. This could be caused by _____.

7. At peak periods everyone's attention should be directed to _____.

8. What is the major offering in the food service business?

12
Your Professional Consultants

For you and your loved ones going into business means investing your money, time and future. For this reason it is well to prepare yourself as much as possible.

Although you may not have had prior experience dealing with bankers, lawyers, accountants, insurance brokers, state and local agencies, now is the time you need their services, to make the decisions that will shape the future of your restaurant business. Many businesses have failed because they were not adequately protected. Here is a list of professional consultants and what each one can do.

BANKERS

1. They can tell you whether or not the landlord, company or franchise is credit worthy—a good or bad risk.

2. Can tell you about the types of financing you may need, such as short-term/long-term borrowing plans, cash flow, secured loans, equipment pledges, chattel mortgages and SBA loans.

3. They will set up a checking account for your business.

SUMMARY: Your banker can explain many things to you, and as he/she is a trusted member of the community in which you plan to do business you should listen, evaluate and respect the opinions and suggestions offered.

LAWYERS

1. A good attorney is worth every penny of his/her fee, especially if he/she has had previous experience with the restaurant business. He/she will set up the legal framework for your business depending on your goals and financial involvement. A law firm can advise you and explain the pros and cons of partnerships, companies, and corporations.

2. Advice and guidance in the negotiations of a lease, or in buying a business, can be a valuable asset in your decision.

3. They can provide you with all the information you need regarding permits, zoning, federal, state and local laws, union information, safety laws, fire codes and total liability.

SUMMARY: Speak to other restaurant owners and find out what they feel their attorney did or didn't do. See your local Small Business Administration agency for information on what an attorney should do for you. Make a checklist. Before you engage an attorney have a clear understanding of the fee, what will be done and when it will be done. Reread this chapter and jot down notes to use when the proper time comes for you to secure the services of an attorney.

INSURANCE BROKERS

1. An insurance broker should give you helpful information about protection from fire, theft, personal inventory, window breakage, employee theft, business disturbances involving loss of sales and general claims.

2. He/she can arrange your own personal life insurance to protect your family in case of your death (to include payments on mortgages, equipment, etc.).

SUMMARY: Compare insurance policies by cost and quality of coverage. Speak to others in the restaurant business to see what they would protect or change if they were just starting in business.

ACCOUNTANT

A major reason for failure in the restaurant business is that many owners/operators have never learned good accounting practices. Yet good accounting practices are just as important as good food! You do not have to be an accounting major to learn the basic principles that will keep your restaurant in business. This is where your accountant comes in. You will be shown how to make clear lists of your expenses. Future trends and expenses must be based on true, realistic figures. If you give an accountant a bunch of slips not properly assigned, the figures will be meaningless. The old accounting expression "garbage in, garbage out" indicates that unless the figures you give an accountant reflect true charges in various categories there is not much that can be done with what there is to work with.

Take the time to fully understand cash on hand sheets, balance sheets, profit and loss statements, inventory closings, posting to ledgers, etc. Do not be afraid to ask questions. Remember that you are paying the accountant to explain things to you, so no question is too silly. It is the accountant's job to help you understand.

Agree on a given time when reports are due to various state and local agencies. Ask what can be set up to keep clear, effective books that provide valuable information to help you guide the future of your business. A daily, simplified accounting procedure can be set up that will let you know where you stand each day. Between you work out a way to keep track of employees' meals, donations, bad debts, bad checks, etc.

FOOD SERVICE CONSULTANTS

A growing new profession is that of the Food Service Consultant. This is a person who has been in the restaurant business for a number of years and understands the complexity of running a successful restaurant. They can be located through local food service, Executive Associations or local Restaurant Association Chapters. Such people can help you evaluate all aspects of your restaurant plan, as well as connect you with the important people and equipment resources you will need. Never be too busy to listen, because the expertise of this person can help you avoid unnecessary problems.

GENERAL SUMMARY

Many people possess specialized knowledge that will be helpful to you in opening your restaurant.   Listen to each and extract those ideas that are useful to you:

Insurance Agencies

They can offer specific information regarding higher premium rates when you locate in a multi-dwelling business block as a tenant with family dwelling above.

Real Estate Brokers

They can show you similar type businesses in other parts of an area compatable in size, surroundings and selling price.

Large Equipment Companies

They have many informative catalogs plus knowledgeable personnel to assist you.

Large Food Companies

They have trained personnel who can teach you how to prepare certain foods.   Some employ dietitians and other specially trained people who naturally promote their products but will also impart much useful information to you.

State Government Agencies (such as Health Departments)

They have speakers, films, pass-out pamphlets and other printed data that can help you.

Federal Agencies

The S.B.A. (Small Business Administration), S.C.O.R.E. (Service Corps of Retired Executives) and A.C.E. (Active Corp. Executives) are all available to give you any help they can.

High Schools and Colleges

They offer evening and weekend courses in bookkeeping, accounting, food service, food service equipment, etc.

QUESTIONS

1. What can a *banker* do to help a prospective restaurant owner?

2. What can a *lawyer* do to help a prospective restaurant owner?

3. What can an *insurance broker* do?

4. What can an *accountant* do?

5. What can a *food service consultant* do?

6. What other places can be contacted for information?

13
Food Service Industry Accounting and Control Forms

Control forms, charts, graphs, plus other forms are a guide in helping you to run and control your business in order to show a profit, year after year. By keeping controls through simple forms, at a later date you can use this information in forecasting purchases, payroll, repairs and other expenses, and control forms will also tell you many other important things regarding your business including what sells, what doesn't sell. All this information can't be remembered by any one person but, if logged in every day at a certain time, it can be used at a later date, and by analyzing the figures this information can be very valuable to you.

The following are suggested forms I would strongly urge you to use once you open. A good idea would also be to consult your accountant or your food service consultant for their suggestions on the forms you plan to use.

One major failure in the food service industry is lack of understanding of basic records kept by owners. They shun them but they are important factors, ranking next to good food, service, etc. Accurate figures, well kept from the beginning are one of the most important steps to success. Your accountant will only be able to give you accurate figures if what you give him is accurate in description, amounts, date, proper charge-off such as repairs, detergents, food, one-time charge, capital expenditures, etc. Your accountant can give you the exact amount of information you need in this area. For example: You can't add soap powder into your cost of food purchases. This is in another category. In order to get the cost of food, repairs, one-time charges, etc. you must keep these expenses separate with the necessary back-up information for them.

CASH REFUND SLIP AND CASH REGISTER PAYMENTS

This type or form of sheet must take care of the situation when a customer wants his/her money back because of dissatisfaction, or when you pay a vendor out of a cash drawer. When you pay for anything out of the register you should have a system whereby you can account for the transaction plus be able to get a signature on the slip. Any good stationery store will provide you with this type of form.

REGISTER CLOSE OUT SHEETS (see page 164) ITEM #1

With your accountant, establish a sheet on how you want to open and close your register daily.

The sample shown is merely a guide and may have to be altered to fit your particular need. Other factors to consider in setting up a register procedure are:

1. Control of all reading items.

2. If money pickups are made at busy times to remove excess bills from the register a slip should be left in the register stating who made the money pickup, the amount, the time and date of the pickup and to where it is being transferred.

3. Leave the register drawer open at closing time. In case of a break-in the register will not be broken if a burglar sees it empty.

4. A count of how many customers you serve a day can be a valuable tool for you. This information can also be taken from your register, daily or hourly.

5. Shortages and overages are apt to happen but you can keep them to a minimum if the following rules are applied: a) Record each sale carefully; b) Be sure your help is trained to make change; c) List all overrings and void; d) If you pay bills out of the register make a notation on the bill paid and last but not least, e) Be ever watchful of the people handling the money. Dishonest employees, once identified, should be dismissed at once.

6. You must make a bank deposit every day. Do *not* make it at the same time each and every day for the obvious reason that you

may be followed and robbed. Use a bank deposit form for this transaction. You will also need a start-off bank which is a certain amount of assorted bills and change to start your business daily.

7. On void sales and overrings, write on the back of the sales check exactly what happened. Control the numerical sequence of each sales check book you issue to each waiter/waitress and compare it to your register detail tape, item for item.

PAYROLL PROCEDURE—TIME CARD, TIME CLOCK, ETC.
(see page 165) ITEM #2

You must set up a system whereby you will pay employees either by check or cash. Your banker or attorney should advise you on the best procedure.

Time clocks or time books are important in the documenting of time worked by employees. Many restaurants use them very successfully. Again, this is an area you will want to be well informed about, because keeping proper documentation of people's time is very important; especially if it has to be checked on at a later date for substantiation.

ACCIDENT REPORT

This is a report form you should keep in the restaurant in case an accident happens to either a customer or to an employee. Your insurance man will advise you how to conduct yourself, and how to fill out the necessary form if a mishap occurs.

WORK CHART (see page 166) ITEM #3

The work charts shown are merely guides.

Next to each job insert the name of the person who will be responsible for seeing that this job is done. You will be adding your own items to the list as time goes on. The list should be posted on the bulletin board for all to see.

CHECKING ACCOUNT

You will have to set up a business checking account. Other items you will be exposed to with your banker and accountant will be

(1) Financial statements and balance sheets, which are no more than the putting together of net worth or capital. (2) Current assets are items that can become cash within a short period or, it is cash you already have. (3) Fixed assets—restaurant equipment is a long-term fixed asset. (4) Current liabilities are debts which are to be paid within one year, as a rule.

You will hear many more terms but, you will find that properly explained, they are not difficult. The big thing is to ask questions until you understand them.

LET YOUR P/L STATEMENT WORK FOR YOU

Your accountant will explain the use of a profit and loss statement as it pertains to your business.

Many successful food service operators analyze the expenses of the past period, determine the reason for any cost increase and then decide what to do to eliminate them in the future.

When you consider that the difference between being in the black or in the red may be only 6-10 percent to 15 percent—it's not that big a spread.

With economic conditions being what they are today, you have to analyze and study all avenues of cost. It's easier to control cost before it spirals than after.

Ask yourself the question "How many sales dollars will I need before I make a profit?" and "How many sales do I need to cover my overhead or break even?"

If costs stay the same they are called fixed expenses. They are called variable if costs vary as sales do.

Example: You do $10,000.00 in sales and your food cost is 42 percent. Food cost should not rise proportionately as food sales increase.

If you do $15,000.00 more in sales the food cost could drop to 40 percent because you should have the following:

1. Less waste.
2. Better utilization of food.
3. Proportionally less cost for all other expenses. The person using the dishwasher will get paid for 8 hours for washing 50 or 100 dishes.

In the same manner if sales drop all other expenses should drop without hurting the remaining sales.

CHECK WRITING

Be sure you have a check writing system in your restaurant. Don't allow any customer to be served without a check. There are many types you can use from a single check to the duplicate system. Whichever you decide to use follow these important suggestions.

1. Issue and control all check books to waiters/waitresses by number.
2. Make sure every slip is accounted for.
3. Match the total slips daily with the total dollar intake as per the register reading.
4. Check the addition, subtraction and selling price on all checks.
5. Use your check slips to fill in your "Meals sold per day" chart.
6. Check on who sells the most, and what foods sell the best. Done on a daily basis this can make money you normally would not take in.
7. Check on who sells more desserts and makes the most suggestions. Suggestion selling adds to the sales of the restaurant.
8. Be sure the customer is presented with the check in a proper manner.
9. Check daily for errors.

DAILY SALES LOG ITEM #4 (see page 167)

It is a good idea to enter each day's sales figures. The daily sales log shown will give you your daily sales to date along with your purchases to give you a daily gross profit percentage.

INVENTORY FORM ITEM #5 (See page 168)

This form is used for taking your inventory weekly, monthly or whenever you wish. It will also give you excellent material to research back months for cost, amounts on hand, etc.

FOOD PURCHASING ITEM #6 (See page 169)

This form filled in daily for food items only will be very valuable to your accountant. Total each column daily after you have entered all vendors' names and the dollar amounts. At the end of the month add up the bottom totals of each day. The actual bills should be filed in an A to Z folder for matching and paying invoices when the vendor asks for payment.

WORK-HOUR REPORT ITEM #7 (see page 170)

This report is necessary to compare the number of hours being worked against the projected volume. Properly analyzed, it can be a valuable tool in knowing when you have too much or too little help on any given day of the week. In this type of planning you must consider the season and the weather for both will affect the volume of business.

WORK SCHEDULE ITEM #8 (see page 171)

A work schedule should be posted so each employee knows when to report for work and when to leave. It may be necessary to post one weekly, in some cases. The schedule shown is only a guide and may have to be altered to fit your needs.

FOOD PREPARATION AND FOOD COST FORM ITEM #9 (see page 172)

This form is used to establish the best possible method of preparing the item step by step. By filling in all the necessary information, i.e. size, portion, unit cost, portion cost, remarks on how the item sells, you will be setting up a standard procedure on how each item is to be made each and every time. You will know your exact cost and will be able to arrive at whatever dollar figure you need to keep your business profitable. You can get help in structuring this from a competent consultant prior to opening your business.

INCOMING DELIVERIES ITEM #10 (see page 173)

This sheet can be a valuable tool in controlling all incoming items. List the asked for information. Keep a separate sheet for each vendor. Compare it with the last delivery amount you were charged. The pack, along with the date, will give you some very important data you can compare day by day and week by week, to see what prices go up and which come down. Check the size packing you are paying for. For example, the first week of any given month you buy a case of carrots, each can weighing 6 lb. 10 oz. (6 cans to a case) and you pay $14.00 per case. Three weeks later you order carrots again and receive cans weighing 6 lb. 2 oz. each. These cost you $16.50 per case. Compare! If you enter your bills daily, you will spot this difference.

PAYROLL COST

When figuring your payroll cost:

1. Try to project your sales in *advance*!
2. Take holidays, weather factor and local conditions into consideration.
3. Take each day of the week, Monday, Tuesday, Wednesday, etc.

   Gross sales per day $400.00
   Labor cost per day $70.00 gross
   Total man hours   40 per day
   Rate per person $1.75 per hour
4. Add everyone's daily gross pay to get your gross dollar cost.
5. Do not use net takehome pay (= after all deductions) amount that you as employer must pay on gross takehome pay (= before any deductions).
6. If your sales are not holding up cut your payroll cost accordingly.

Tips to Control Payroll Costs

a. Analyze each job to be done for need.
b. Match the person to the job.
c. Post an accurate schedule. Cross-check the hours.
d. Break down the number of customers served by each waiter/ waitress daily, weekly, etc.
e. Budget your payroll dollar cost to your estimated sales.

ITEM #2.

Time Card ___   Week Ending ___

Social Security No. ___   Employee Name ___

Job Description	In	Meals		Out	Daily Total	Auth.
		Out	In			
		Sat.				
		Sun.				
		Mon.				
		Tues.				
		Wed.				
		Thu.				
		Fri.				
Summary						Weekly Total
Regular	X-Time	Sick	Vac.	Other		
						Weekly Total
Approval						

Item #3. Work Chart

1. Back of kitchen in good order.
2. All trash removed.
3. Rest rooms clean and in order.
4. Uniforms in hamper.
5. Sink and drain boards clean.
6. Refrigerator and shelves in good order.
7. Refrigerator temperature recorded.
8. Stock shelves and paper supplies.
9. Fryers on proper fat level and at correct temperature.
10. Adequate supply of carry-out bags on hand.
11. Coffee maker clean and coffee made.
12. Hot and cold cup dispensers full. Have back-up supplies ready when rush starts.
13. Napkin and straw containers in place and full.
14. Cream dispenser clean, full and ready to go.
15. Slicer clean and sharp.
16. Scales clean—portion weight checked.
17. Customer area clean, napkin dispensers full, ash trays clean.
18. Inside trash containers clean—liners in place.
19. Outside area clean—trash containers in place.
20. Cash bank in register and ready to go.

Item #4: Daily Sales Log.

Day of Month	Daily Sales (A)	Daily Purchases (B)	Sales to Date (C)	Purchases to Date (D)	Gross Profit (E)
1					
2					
3					
4					
5					
6					
7					
8					
9					
10					
11					
12					
13					
14					
15					
16					
17					
18					
19					
20					
21					
22					
23					
24					
25					
26					
27					
28					
29					
30					
31					

1. Enter sales (cumulative in Section (C)).
2. Subtract cumulative purchases in Section (D).
3. Subtract (D) from (C). This gives you Section (E).
4. Divide Section (C) into Section (E) which gives you your gross percentage for the day.

Item #5. Inventory Form

Taken By:

For Ordering Etc.	Quantity		Unit lb.–Doz. #10, etc.	Description	Cost Unit	Cost Total
	Stock Room Kitchen	Total Count				

Item #6: Food Purchases.

Date ___

Initial ___

Vendor	1	2	3	4	5	6	7	8	9	10	11	12	13	14	15	16	17	18	19	20	21	22	23	24	25	26	27	28	29	30	31	Total

Item #7. Work Hours Report

Week Ending

Work Hours Schedule	Mon.	Tues.	Wed.	Thurs.	Fri.	Sat.	Sun.	
Projected Sales								Total
Employee's Name								
Number of Customers Served								
Projected Daily Hours								
Projected Payroll Dollars								
Projected Percentage								
Actual Sales								
Actual Daily Payroll Dollars								
Actual Hours								

Item #8: Work Schedule.

Week Beginning

Name	Employee's Initial	Monday In	Monday Out	Tuesday In	Tuesday Out	Wednesday In	Wednesday Out	Thursday In	Thursday Out	Friday In	Friday Out	Saturday In	Saturday Out	Sunday In	Sunday Out	Total Hrs./Wk.

Item #9. Food Preparation and Food Cost Form

Date

Item	Size Portion	Unit Cost	Portion Cost

Comments	Cost _____ Add 10% Shrinkage_____ Finished Cost_____ Selling Price_____ Deduct Finished Cost _____ Gross Profit_____ Gross %_____
Preparation Method	

Item #10: Incoming Deliveries.

USE ONE SHEET FOR EACH COMPANY

Date Rec'd	List All Supplies Name	Quantity Received	Unit Price		Amount of Invoice or Del. Slip	Charge Purch.	Cash Purch.
			Price	Per Lb.			

QUESTIONS

1. What are reasons for using control forms?

2. What are some of the factors to consider in setting up a register procedure?

3. What are (1) current assets and (2) fixed assets?

4. List some of the suggestions to consider in check writing.

5. What is a "Food Cost Test Form" used for?

6. What can be done to control payroll costs?

14
Sanitation and Safety

Sanitation Does Influence Sales This cannot be repeated too many times. Check the following things carefully.

FLOORS, WALLS AND CEILINGS

From cellar and/or storage area to kitchen preparation area, serving areas, lobbies and rest rooms, the floors, walls and ceilings should be clean and in good repair. *Floors* should be smooth, tightly laid and washed as often as necessary for safety's sake as well as for health reasons. Drains should be cleaned regularly and if mats are used they should be easy to move for cleaning purposes. *Walls* (including doors and windows) and *ceilings* should be washable and kept free of dust, grease and cobwebs. They should also be constructed to prevent insects and dust from getting into cracks.

LIGHTING AND VENTILATION

All areas should be well lighted and ventilated. Any ventilation system used must comply with state and local fire prevention requirements.

GARBAGE AND PEST CONTROL

One way to prevent flies, rats, roaches, etc. from invading the premises is to make sure garbage is properly handled. Containers must be leak-proof, have tight fitting covers and be nonabsorbent. After emptying, they should be washed thoroughly, inside and out. All areas where food is stored and prepared must be kept spotless to prevent the breeding of any vermin.

When breaking down a customer's table, dishes, silverware and garbage should go into separate bus boxes. This creates less of a problem when plates are scraped prior to being washed.

STORAGE

Racks or dollies should be used in storing cases, bags, or other containers of food. This makes cleaning easier and protects them from being splashed when floor is washed. Canned food that does not need washing, or food that does not require cooking, should be stored away from other food to prevent contamination. Keep poisonous or toxic substances, such as cleaning fluids or pesticides out of food storage areas.

FOOD PROTECTION

From the time food is delivered until the time it is served it can be kept free from contamination by 1) maintaining correct temperature in storeroom, freezers, and display cases; 2) placing food in refrigerators so air can circulate freely and keeping refrigerated foods protected so foreign objects will not accidentally fall in; 3) not leaving food out in kitchen any longer than necessary during preparation; 4) keeping hot food hot and cold food cold.

Wash fruits and vegetables thoroughly whether they are to be served cooked or raw. Use proper utensils during preparation of food and for food put out for cafeteria-type service, buffets, etc. especially unwrapped or uncovered food so manual contact by employees or customers will be kept at a minimum. Use tongs, forks, spoons, etc. wherever possible. Protect food in cafeteria-type service, buffets, etc. from contamination by using counter-protector devices or containers that do an effective job and are easily cleaned.

MILK AND MILK PRODUCTS

All states have regulations regarding use of fluid milk, manufactured milk products and other fluid dairy products. These regulations must be followed.

WASHING AND STERILIZING FACILITIES

Make sure all plumbing, including dishwashers and garbage disposals, is properly installed and that a constant supply of hot water is available at peak periods. Check Health Department's requirement in your area for wash and rinse water temperature. Change water in dishwasher frequently. If using an automatic detergent feeder make sure it is working properly. Check the time that utensils are exposed to washing and sterilizing process. Keep landing tables clean.

EMPLOYEES' PERSONAL HYGIENE

Employees handling food or food-contact surfaces must practice good personal hygiene while at work; clean uniforms, fingernails clean and trimmed, clean hair kept in place by head piece or hairnet, hands washed with soap and warm water before starting work, as often as necessary during working hours and always after using toilet facilities. Do not allow them to work if they have a communicable disease, open sores, a cold, etc.

Disease-carrying Germs

A germ is a microorganism that is found everywhere. One germ can reproduce over a trillion in a day's time. Some of these are harmless, some are useful but many are extremely dangerous. Freezing will slow down their growth while high temperatures will kill them. Germs grow quickly at body temperature. Disease-carrying germs in food or water can cause: a) food infections *from* food contaminated by flies, rats, unwashed hands, or work surfaces and utensils not cleaned thoroughly after each use. This can cause a severe upset 12 to 24 hours after eating. This is called Salmonella. (b) Food infections can also be caused by people having boils or open, infected sores. This is known as Staphylococcus and can cause violent illness from 3 to 12 hours after eating. (c) Bacillary dysentery is brought on by food handled with unwashed hands or by flies. Dishes, glasses, etc. can be contaminated by a carrier. This can also be caused by using water that is not clean at its source. This bacteria is known as Shigella. (d) Septic sore throat is caused by coughing, sneezing or spitting. This can also be caused by raw milk that was contaminated at the source. This bacteria is known as Streptococcus. It is usually humans that cause food poisoning by transferring disease-carrying germs to food or water.

Employees may have to be reminded 1) not to cough or sneeze near food or dishes; 2) to keep fingers out of glasses and cups; 3) to always pick forks, spoons and knives up by the handles and 4) to *never* reuse any food left by customers.

SUMMARY: Sanitation performance is one of the most important aspects of the food service industry. A potential health hazard is always present when dealing with perishable products that are to be consumed. Eliminate this hazard by always practicing good sanitation procedures.

Health departments throughout the country are staffed with professional people. Go over your equipment layout with them early in the planning stage.

FIRE PREVENTION

Many buildings have been destroyed due to fires starting in kitchen or grill sections. Have a regular procedure established which is to be followed to make sure a fire doesn't put you out of business.

1. Have someone responsible for checking kitchen and grill areas regularly, making sure they are clean and free of grease at all times.

2. If you have filters, get them cleaned on a regular basis (preferably weekly). Failure to do this is a prime cause of many restaurant fires.

3. Exhaust ducts must be kept clean. Have a reliable firm do this.

4. Contact the local fire department and ask for their opinion on the kind of fire fighting equipment you should have in your restaurant. Follow their advice.

5. All restaurants must have at least two exits, clearly visible to customers and employees alike (larger restaurants would naturally have more than two).

6. If you have any gas appliances in your establishment, check periodically to make sure all pipes, joints, etc. are tight with no gas leakage. There should be an outside shutoff in case of an emergency.

7. Most cities and towns have someone in charge of checking any major electrical installations. Contact them, before opening day, so you can rest assured that electrical work has been done properly.

8. Employees should be instructed in fire prevention as part of their training. Remind them that, in case of a fire, customers should be helped to leave premises quickly but without panic.

9. Preventing fires is everyone's responsibility. By using common sense, always using gas and/or electrical equipment properly and by observing all safety rules, a tragedy can be averted.

10. Don't let poor housekeeping, careless smoking or any other negligent act cause a fire in your restaurant.

RESPONSIBILITY FOR PUBLIC SAFETY

Steps should be taken by the owner/operator of a restaurant to guard against customer accidents in his place of business.

1. Anything spilled on the floor should be cleaned up immediately. Floor should be mopped and dried well, especially if it is greasy. Wet floors are the major cause of many customer falls.

2. Mats placed inside main entrance can help prevent falls during periods of bad weather.

3. Any loose floor tiles or rugs that do not lay flat should be replaced immediately.

4. Wet mopping of floors should be done after closing time, if possible. If it must be done during business hours, make sure it is not done at peak periods. As each area is washed it should also be dry mopped at once, and "A" frame floor signs used.

5. Chairs, tables, stools, etc. should be checked for splinters, and legs or bases that are unsteady or uneven should be replaced.

RULES FOR EMPLOYEES' SAFETY

The time element involved in preparing meals on schedule is inclined to make some workers take unnecessary chances in their haste to get things done. Haste not only makes waste—it can also cause injuries. These can be avoided if the proper and safe procedures are followed:

1.   Some of the equipment used in restaurant kitchens today can cause injury if not used properly.

2.   All employees using any kind of electrical appliances (slicers, mixers, dishwashers, etc.) should be thoroughly trained in their use before being allowed to operate them.   The manager and/or cook should be alert and watch for anyone not using proper safety procedures; for example: not using guards on equipment such as slicers; using fingers near moving parts of mixers, slicers, etc.

3.   Dishroom attendants or those cleaning off trays in dishroom should always keep glassware, plates and silverware separate to avoid breakage.   If glassware or china does get broken, sweep it up at once. Do *not* pick up with fingers.   Any china or glassware found to be chipped should be disposed of.

4.   Those working around steamers, steam tables, or coffee urns should be extremely careful in opening doors, changing pans or removing covers.   Steam burns can be very serious.

5.   In the kitchen, as in the dining room, spills should be taken care of immediately.   Workers carrying pots or trays can very easily slip on a wet or greasy area they did not see and be seriously injured.

6.   Comfortable, sensible, low-heeled shoes are a must for all workers.

7.   The door from kitchen area into dining room should have a window so collisions of those going in and coming out may be avoided.   If there is a double door, one door should only swing in and the other should only swing out so there is no chance of people on opposite sides trying to go through the same door at the same time. Also a posted sign will help.

QUESTIONS

1.   Sanitation does ____ does not ____ influence sales.

2.   When checking a cellar, what should you look for?

3.   What should be checked in washing and sterilizing facilities?

4.   Why must food be kept covered in the refrigerator?

5.   What should you do when handling glasses or cups?

6. Food left by customers must be returned to kitchen for re-use.

   True ____   False ____

7. What should you have and use for every piece of equipment?

8. Why is sanitation so important to food service industry?

9. What agency should be contacted early in planning?

10. Give two reasons why a cook or baker might become irritable.

11. What should the owner/manager do to prevent employees from becoming irritable?

12. List five ways to prevent fires from starting.

13. What steps should be taken to prevent customer accidents?

14. List five rules that should be followed for employees' safety.

15
Merchandising
in Food Service

What is merchandising in food service? Actually, food service merchandising is the portion of your business that involves your customer the most and has a direct reflection upon sales. In order to have a successful merchandising program, you must start with the location of your business, the decor inside and out and the actual dishes the food is served on. Food *must* be attractive. You've heard it said that people first eat with their eyes. Your menu, silverware, glassware, china, lighting, employee's uniforms, etc. are all part of merchandising in food service.

Food Merchandising is the effective putting together of all these support features to induce sales and keep people coming back. Following is a list of suggested merchandising techniques in food service:

1. A good restaurant operator is constantly looking for ways to present a product better. One manager wanted to serve a hamburger in some way other than on a hamburger roll. He came up with the following: "Hamburger Club Special" which was three slices of toasted bread—a hamburger on one slice of toast, lettuce and tomato on another slice and mayonnaise on the third slice. He stacked all the items together, put large, fancy tooth picks through the stacks, cut it into four sections, served it on a beautiful round wood platter and served it with potato chips and pickles. He was able to get a higher unit price by incorporating the lettuce, tomatoes and potato chips and was also able to offer something different to his customers. Serving this on the wood platter was the little extra touch that customers appreciate.

2. Some food service businesses now offer what is called the "Half N Half Sandwich." One half is pastrami and the other is corned beef. This is another form of food merchandising.

3. Placemats with information of local historical interest to the reader is another excellent idea.

4. Parsley with sandwiches and dinners also does an excellent job of adding color to a dish.

5. Paprika on mashed potatoes also gives eye appeal to a plate offering.

6. One good way to merchandise freshly made salads, pudding, watermelon, pies, cakes, etc. is to place them in a display case in full view of the customer, with a light directly over them. This will pay off in added sales.

7. Displays, attention to special times of year, holidays, etc. can all be used to merchandise your business to the best advantage.

8. One restaurant had all its employees wear a special pin announcing a new banquet room they were just opening. This invited questions from the customers, which led to a successful opening of the new room.

9. Baker's dozen—giving 13 items and charging for 12, is another merchandising scheme.

10. Menus must be clean at all times. Nothing can hurt your overall attempt at good food merchandising than to present a dirty or barely readable menu to your customers.

11. Special dessert menus, liquor menus, flyers, salad menus are all excellent methods to enhance your merchandising efforts.

SUMMARY: In food service merchandising we now know that along with good food must come many other support items. These ultimately lead to keeping the customer interested, through the total food service merchandising program, to return time and again to your restaurant.

QUESTIONS

1. What is food merchandising?

2. What are some of the things to consider in order to have a successful merchandising program?

3. What is a baker's dozen?

4. Good food along with special merchandising techniques will lead to ___.

16
Getting Set Up
for Opening Day

Opening any business is difficult and will always have unexpected problems.

Some statements, some questions and some suggestions are:

1. After you are open for awhile review what you have accomplished. After two or three weeks, see if your sales are in line with your expenses. The problem is that people going into business want to give good service and will often over staff and fail to level off later on.

2. When you open, forget everything else; your hobbies, clubs, etc. and stick with the business 100 percent. Learn about every problem in it. Get to know every person's abilities and weaknesses (managers, cooks, waitresses/waiters, etc.)

3. Opening day will tell how well you planned and can give you a following and a reputation.

4. Train yourself to watch peoples' facial expressions. This can tell you if they're satisfied. Walk around, talk to the customers, smile, be interested in them; however, don't hold too long a conversation with anyone. Just let them know you are interested in their impression of the service, the food and their likes and dislikes. You want to do well so anything they can say to help you will be appreciated. Let them know that their comments mean a lot to you as the owner of a new establishment.

5. Some of your less popular friends are sure to come in. Be diplomatic no matter how hard it may be to do so.

6. Watch cash handling especially on the first day. Be sure you collect for all your services. Keep an eye on all side doors, rear entrances, etc.

7. Tell your suppliers that you may need emergency delivery of goods. Know how to get in touch with them in case you need merchandise, food, repairs to your equipment in a hurry.

8. Write clearly and post on your bulletin board all emergency telephone numbers (police, fire department, employees' home phones, suppliers, your own home phone).

9. Look for reasons to praise your employees especially on opening day. This creates the desire for them to do a good job.

10. Help to build team spirit by working along with your employees.

11. Assign waiters/waitresses certain responsibilities. Tell them who is to take care of what, when and how.

12. If you have to correct your help do it in a quiet manner. Remember that opening day is rough!

13. Handle complaints gracefully and correct them immediately. If the customer says, "This turkey is cold" the employee should respond, "I'm sorry. Let me get you a hot dinnner right away." Remember that the customer is always right so be gracious.

Consider the following:

a. Did you think to hire extra help?

b. Can you get nickles, dimes, etc. on Saturday, Sunday, nights? Where?

c. Do you have a plan in case a key person quits on the first or second day?

d. What will happen if you are sick on opening day? Does everyone know the menu in order to answer any questions?

e. Did you teach everyone how to make every item on the menu? Do they know how it should be cooked?

f. Someone once said "It costs money to advertise." This is true but it is a necessary thing, however, open quietly the first week. Get all the problems, help, equipment, supplies and other problems solved and then advertise.

g. Do you have every item on the menu available and ready?

h. Have you covered all areas with your lawyer, accountant and consultant? Do they think you are ready to open?

i. Don't overstock supplies, food, etc. Get daily deliveries at first.

j. Have you all the licenses you need? Insurance?

k. Who is to clean rest rooms, parking lot?

l. Is the telephone installed?

m. Do you have someone you can call in case of a major power failure? Are extra electrical fuses available?

n. Does everyone know where all shut-offs are? (water, gas, heat, etc.)

o. Did you plan for credit cards and extra register tapes for back-up?

p. Burglar alarm.

q. Do you know how to work all equipment? If equipment breaks down on the first day, can you get it serviced in a hurry?

SUMMARY: Many things need to be considered when you plan for opening day. Things will go wrong no matter how well you have planned. If you use a clipboard with a pad and go through each area of your business jotting down all things that must be accomplished in order to open, many potential problems will be eliminated.

Meet with your employees, lawyer, insurance agent, banker and consultant. Write down all suggestions they offer and as they are accomplished cross them off your list.

With all this going on you will feel more physical and emotional pressure than usual. Make sure you are in good health. Try to keep calm at home, in spite of the additional burden and stress placed on you and your family at this time.

Choose your help wisely and allow only reliable persons the privilege of opening and closing the restaurant. Trust only a few with the key to your business.

Remember that as soon as you open the door you will start creating an impression with your help, customers, suppliers, etc.

You must handle mistakes by your employees on the spot—correct, train and rectify mistakes as they are made. Informed help provide efficient service. Display a bulletin board and train your help to read it daily. Get into the habit of posting all specific information pertaining to menu changes, suggestions to pass on to the customers, etc.

During the busy hours remove excess bills from the cash register. Keep an eye out for walk outs, who either can't be served immediately or try to leave without paying.

Be sure all stations are covered and that waiters/waitresses do not feed their friends without charging them. It is possible to occasionally have a dishonest employee. One of the best ways to prevent this is to have employees prove themselves. Later, let them know how well they are doing or in what ways they can improve.

QUESTIONS

1. After the restaurant is open for awhile what should owner/operator do?

2. What should you know about every person working for you?

3. Why should you talk with customers?

4. What information should be posted on bulletin board?

5. How should complaints be handled?

6. List some of points that should be considered before opening.

7. When should employees' mistakes be corrected?

17
Checklist of
Things to be Done in
Setting Up a New Business

REGISTRATION OF TRADE NAME

Make application for a business permit and registration of trade or business name. The cost is minimal but may vary from state to state. Apply at City or Town Hall where you live or where your principal place of business will be located. Always check with the City or Town Hall. Many communities do not require any type of permit. Even if they do not and you are the sole proprietor always register the name under which you will do business with the City or Town Clerk if it is different from your own name. State laws usually require that you register the business name or you will be fined.

STATEWIDE

The sale of tobacco, liquor, handling of food, etc. is governed by a number of laws and regulations.
NEVER ATTEMPT TO START ANY BUSINESS WITHOUT CHECKING ALL STATE, CITY OR TOWN REGULATIONS *BEFORE* DOING BUSINESS.

ZONING LAWS

Always check the local zoning laws before attempting to start a business even if you have been told it is zoned for the type of business you want. Better to be safe than sorry—out of money and out of business.

WORKMENS' COMPENSATION LAWS

Any business person who hires three or more employees must purchase Workmens' Compensation Insurance. The Department of Labor in each state enforces this law. This insurance provides for medical payments and weekly wage replacement benefits for those employees injured on the job. This insurance can be purchased from any insurance company. Cost of the insurance depends on the degree of hazards attributed to the employee's job, safety of employer's premises, etc.

TAXATION

As sole proprietor, with or without employees, you must apply for a permit to sell at retail. Cost may vary from state to state. Apply at your State Division of Taxation. If you have employees you must register with the State Division of Taxation for an Employer's Identification Number. You must also apply for a Federal Employer's Identification Number at the office of the Internal Revenue Service.

DEPARTMENT OF LABOR

You will have to pay into the Employment Security Fund as an employer. The amount you have to pay will depend on the rate of turnover you have with employees. For example as of this writing: In Rhode Island this amount is 2.7 percent to 3.7 percent and is on the first $4,800.00 paid in a calendar year. This amount varies in different states so make sure you check what percentage it is in your state. Also check the amount you must deduct from employee's wages for temporary disability insurance. All states do not have this and rates, where applicable, are subject to change, so check with appropriate authority.

STATE INCOME TAX

You must withhold on each pay day, from wages paid, a percentage of the Federal Income Tax withheld and pay this on a regular basis to the State Division of Taxation. This percentage is another thing that varies from state to state. Check it out.

SOCIAL SECURITY CARDS

All employees must have a Social Security card. It must be signed by its owner and you should always ask to see it and personally record the social security number. Failure to do so may cause your employee to lose benefits and cause considerable trouble for you in back tracking to uncover any errors.

DEDUCTIONS

Each pay day, your employees must receive a statement from you telling them what deductions were made and how many dollars were taken out for each legal purpose. This can be on the check as a detachable portion or in the form of an envelope with the items printed and spaces for dollar deductions to be filled in.

No deductions may be made by any employer for any reason unless the employee has previously signed a paper authorizing the deduction. THERE ARE NO EXCEPTIONS TO THIS.

FEDERAL INCOME TAX

Like the State Income Tax, the method of paying Federal Income Taxes depends upon your legal form of business. The following procedures must be followed:

Sole Proprietorship

You must file a Federal Schedule C along with your personal Federal Income Tax Return (Form 1040) and any other applicable forms pertaining to your gains or losses in your business activity.

Partnership

You must file a Federal Partnership return (Form 1065). This is merely informational to show gross and net earnings of P & L. Also, each partner must report his share of the partnership earnings on his individual Form 1040.

Corporation

You must file a Federal Corporation Income Tax return (Form 1120).
You will also be required to file an individual return on your earnings from the corporation.

FEDERAL PAYROLL TAXES

Federal Withholding Tax

Any business that employs a person other than himself must register
with the IRS and acquire an employer identification number and pay
Federal Withholding Tax, at least quarterly.   File Form SS-4 with
IRS to obtain number and required tax forms.

Federal Insurance Contribution Act (FICA)

Any businessperson who employs even one person must pay the
current rate of 5.85% of employee's gross income, up to $16,500.00
for employee's Social Security Benefits. If self-employed he/she just
pays 7.90%.   The employee then contributes 5.85% for a combined
rate of 11.7% of gross income.

Both of these withholdings (Federal Withholding Tax and FICA
Tax) result in a requirement for preparing the W-2 Form for each
employee.   The W-2 Form is due once a year and must be prepared,
mailed and received by the employee before January 31st of the
following year.

Federal Unemployment Tax Act (FUTA)

The employer must contribute 3.4% of the employee's gross wages
up to $4,200.00 in any given year.   Form 940 must be prepared and
paid by January 31st of the following year.

Special Forms

You must retain either the W-4 Form from employees so that they
can show you how much they claim for deductions and what to

withhold, or the special form for those whose wages will not reach $750.00 annually, such as part-time students.

Depository Form

You must deposit in your bank on a "Depository" form each pay day if you are required to withhold more than $100.00 on any pay day. IRS has these forms for you. Ask for the "Mr. Businessman's Kit." The kit has sample forms.

BUSINESS INSURANCE

In another section we have discussed the owner's business *life* insurance. You also have to consider the various types of insurance needed to protect your business. These include: Fire, Liability, Burglary, Accident, Employees' Union insurance, just to name a few.

Fire Insurance

The small business people *must* have enough fire insurance to cover a complete loss. They cannot afford less, as in most cases, they have invested all available capital in the business. It would be foolhardy to think that it could not happen to you. Without adequate fire insurance you could lose your business if there was a fire and you would still have outstanding bills to pay. If your business is in an area where severe storms, tornadoes, etc. are apt to occur your insurance should also include this coverage.

Liability Insurance

There are many types of liability insurance you should consider. If your restaurant is in a rented or leased building liability insurance will be insisted on by the landlord. If a customer should fall, trip or is injured in some other way while on the premises; the furnace explodes (causing someone to be hurt) or backfires (causing the inside of restaurant to be covered with soot) or someone or something breaks a window, someone could be injured or the furnishings could be damaged and the landlord would be responsible unless you have this coverage.

Burglary Insurance

You have already been warned never to leave money in the restaurant overnight, but someone planning a robbery won't know that. There are other things they could steal, such as cash registers, typewriters, kitchen equipment and utensils. Paying for this insurance would be cheaper than having to replace items stolen.

Accident Insurance

You want to be covered in case of an accident to one of your employees. This could be caused by someone's carelessness or by a piece of equipment. Did you know you could be held responsible if one of your employees was going to make a bank deposit and was injured in an accident?

EMPLOYEES' UNION INSURANCE

This is covered by Workman's Compensation, which is something you must pay into if your employees belong to a union. This covers them only while they are working and anything that happens outside of working hours is not covered by this insurance and you are not responsible.

HELPFUL INFORMATION

On the following pages you will find the names, addresses and telephone numbers of various agencies that you might wish to contact for additional information:

1. Small Business Administration offices.
2. U.S. Dept. of Transportation-Federal Railroad Administration.
3. U.S. Dept. of Commerce-Economic Development Administration.
4. U.S. Dept. of Agriculture-Farmers Home Administration.

Included at the end of this chapter is a metric conversion table. The United States is in the process of changing to this system so it would be well for you to become familiar with it.

SBA FIELD OFFICES: ADDRESSES AND TELEPHONE NUMBERS

REGION		CITY	STATE	ZIP CODE	ADDRESS	(TELEPHONE NUMBERS FOR PUBLIC USE ONLY)
I	RO	Boston	Mass.	02114	150 Causeway St., 10th Floor	(617) 223-2100
	DO	Boston	Mass.	02114	150 Causeway St., 10th Floor	(617) 223-2100
	POD	Holyoke	Mass.	01040	302 High Street - 4th Floor	(413) 536-8770
	DO	Augusta	Maine	04330	Federal Building, 40 Western Ave., Room 512	(207) 622-6171
	DO	Concord	N.H.	03301	55 Pleasant St., Room 213	(603) 224-4041
	DO	Hartford	Conn.	06103	One Financial Plaza	(203) 244-3600
	DO	Montpelier	Vt.	05602	Federal Building, 87 State St., Room 210	(802) 223-7472
	DO	Providence	R.I.	02903	57 Eddy St., Room 7th Fl	(401) 528-1000
II	RO	New York	N.Y.	10007	26 Federal Plaza, Room 3214	(212) 264-1468
	DO	New York	N.Y.	10007	26 Federal Plaza, Room 3100	(212) 264-4355
	POD	Melville	N.Y.	11746	425 Broad Hollow Rd., Rm. 205	(516) 752-1626
	DO	Hato Rey	Puerto Rico	00919	Chardon and Bolivia Streets, P.O. Box 1915	(809) 763-6363
	POD	St. Thomas	Virgin Island	00801	Franklin Building	(809) 774-1331
	DO	Newark	N.J.	07102	970 Broad St., Room 1635	(201) 645-2434
	POD	Camden	N.J.	08104	1800 East Davis Street	(609) 757-5183
	DO	Syracuse	N.Y.	13202	Federal Building-Room 1073- 100 South Clinton Street	(315) 473-3314
	BO	Buffalo	N.Y.	14202	111 West Huron St., Room 1311, Federal Building	(716) 842-3240
	BO	Elmira	N.Y.	14901	180 State Street - Rm. 412	(607) 733-4686
	POD	Albany	N.Y.	12210	99 Washington Ave., Twin Towers Bldg., Room 921	(518) 472-6300
	POD	Rochester	N.Y.	14614	Federal Building, 100 State Street	(716) 263-6700

196

SBA FIELD OFFICES: ADDRESSES AND TELEPHONE NUMBERS (cont'd)

REGION		CITY	STATE	ZIP CODE	ADDRESS	(TELEPHONE NUMBERS FOR PUBLIC USE ONLY)
	RO	Philadelphia	Bala Cynwyd, Pa.	19004	231 St. Asaphs Rd., 1 Bala Cynwyd Plaza, Suite 646 West Lobby	(215) 597-3311
	DO	Philadelphia	Bala Cynwyd, Pa.	19004	231 St. Asaphs Rd., 1 Bala Cynwyd Plaza, Suite 400 East Lobby	(215) 597-3311
	BO	Harrisburg	Pa.	17102	1500 North 2nd Street	(717) 782-3840
	BO	Wilkes-Barre	Pa.	18702	Penn Place, 20 N. Pennsylvania Ave.	(717) 826-6497
	BO	Wilmington	Del.	19801	844 King Street, Federal Building. Rm 5207 - Lockbox 16	(302) 571-6294
III	DO	Baltimore	Towson, Md.	21204	7800 York Rd.	(301) 962-2150
	DO	Clarksburg	W. Va.	26301	109 North 3rd St., Room 301, Lowndes Building	(304) 623-5631
	BO	Charleston	W. Va.	25301	Charleston National Plaza, Suite 628	(304) 343-6181
	DO	Pittsburgh	Pa.	15222	Federal Building, 1000 Liberty Ave., Room 1401	(412) 644-2780
	DO	Richmond	Va.	23240	Federal Building, 400 North 8th St., Room 3015	(804) 782-2617
	DO	Washington	D.C.	20417	1030 15th St. N.W. Suite 250	(202) 655-4000
	RO	Atlanta	Ga.	30309	1401 Peachtree St., N.E., Room 470	(404) 881-4943
	DO	Atlanta	Ga.	30309	1720 Peachtree Street, N.E., 6th Floor	(404) 881-4325
IV	DO	Birmingham	Ala.	35205	908 South 20th St., Room 202	(205) 254-1344
	DO	Charlotte	N.C.	28202	230 S. Tryon Street	(704) 372-0711
	POD	Greenville	N.C.	27834	215 South Evans Street Rm. 206	(919) 752-3798

SBA FIELD OFFICES: ADDRESSES AND TELEPHONE NUMBERS (cont'd)

REGION	CITY	STATE	ZIP CODE	ADDRESS	(TELEPHONE NUMBERS FOR PUBLIC USE ONLY)
DO	Columbia	S.C.	29201	1801 Assembly St., Room 131	(803) 765-5376
DO	Jackson	Miss.	39201	Petroleum Bldg., Suite 690, 200 E. Pascagoula St.	(601) 969-4371
BO	Biloxi	Miss.	39530	111 Fred Haise Blvd., Gulf Nat. Life Insurance Bldg. 2nd Floor	(601) 435-3676
DO	Jacksonville	Fla.	32202	Federal Building, 400 West Bay St. Room 261, PO Box 35067	(904) 791-3782
DO	Louisville	Ky.	40201	Federal Building, 600 Federal Pl., Room 188	(502) 582-5971
IV DO	Miami	Coral Gables, Fla.	33134	2222 Ponce De Leon Blvd., 5th Floor	(305) 350-5521
POD	Tampa	Fla.	33607	1802 N. Trask Street, Suite 203	(813) 228-2594
DO	Nashville	Tenn.	37219	404 James Robertson Parkway, Suite 1012	(615) 749-5881
BO	Knoxville	Tenn.	37902	502 South Gay St., Room 307, Fidelity Bankers Building	(615) 637-9300
POD	Memphis	Tenn.	38103	Federal Building, 167 North Main St., Room 211	(901) 521-3588
POD	West Palm Beach	Fla.	33402	Federal Building, 701 Clematis St., Room 229	(305) 659-7533
RO	Chicago	Ill.	60604	Federal Building, 219 South Dearborn St., Room 838	(312) 353-0355
V DO	Chicago	Ill.	60604	Federal Building, 219 South Dearborn St., Room 437	(312) 353-4528
BO	Springfield	Ill.	62701	One North, Old State Capital Plaza	(217) 525-4416

SBA FIELD OFFICES: ADDRESSES AND TELEPHONE NUMBERS (cont'd)

REGION		CITY	STATE	ZIP CODE	ADDRESS	(TELEPHONE NUMBERS FOR PUBLIC USE ONLY)
	DO	Cleveland	Ohio	44199	1240 East 9th St., Room 317	(216) 522-4180
	DO	Columbus	Ohio	43215	34 North High Street, Tonti Bldg.	(614) 469-6860
	BO	Cincinnati	Ohio	45202	Federal Building, 550 Main St.	(513) 684-2814
	DO	Detroit	Mich.	48226	477 Michigan Ave., McNamara Building	(313) 226-6075
	BO	Marquette	Mich.	49855	540 W. Kaye Ave., Don H. Bottum University Center	(906) 225-1108
V	DO	Indianapolis	Ind.	46204	575 North Pennsylvania St., Rm. 552 New Fed. Bldg.	(317) 269-7272
	DO	Madison	Wis.	53703	122 West Washington Ave., Room 713	(608) 252-5261
	BO	Milwaukee	Wis.	53233	735 West Wisconsin Ave., Room 690, Continental Bank Bldg.	(414) 224-3941
	POD	Eau Claire	Wis.	54701	500 South Barstow St., Room B9AA, Fed. Off. Bldg. & U.S. Courthouse	(715) 834-9012
	DO	Minneapolis	Minn.	55402	12 South 6th St., Plymouth Building	(612) 725-2362
	RO	Dallas	Tex.	75235	1720 Regal Row, Regal Park Office Bldg., Suite 230	(214) 749-2531
VI	DO	Dallas	Tex.	75202	1100 Commerce St., Room 300	(214) 749-1011
	POD	Marshall	Tex.	75670	100 South Washington Street, Federal Building G-12	(214) 935-5257
	DO	Albuquerque	N. Mex.	87110	5000 Marble Ave., N.E., Patio Plaza Bldg.	(505) 766-3430
	DO	Houston	Tex.	77002	One Allen Ctr, 500 Dallas	(713) 226-4341

SBA FIELD OFFICES: ADDRESSES AND TELEPHONE NUMBERS (cont'd)

REGION		CITY	STATE	ZIP CODE	ADDRESS	(TELEPHONE NUMBERS FOR PUBLIC USE ONLY)
	DO	Little Rock	Ark.	72201	611 Gaines St., Suite 900	(501) 378-5871
	DO	Lubbock	Tex.	79408	1205 Texas Ave., 712 Federal Office Bldg. & U.S. Courthouse	(806) 762-7011
	BO	El Paso	Tex.	79901	4100 Rio Bravo, Suite 300	(915) 543-7200
	DO	Lower Rio Grande Valley	Harlingen, Tex.	78550	222 East Van Buren Street	(512) 423-3011
VI	BO	Corpus Christi	Tex.	78408	3105 Leopard St.	(512) 888-3011
	DO	New Orleans	La.	70113	1001 Howard Ave., Plaza Tower, 17th Floor	(504) 589-2611
	POD	Shreveport	La.	71163	Fannin Street, U.S. Post Office & Courthouse Building	(318) 226-5196
	DO	Oklahoma City	Okla.	73118	50 Penn Place, Suite 840	(405) 736-4011
	DO	San Antonio	Tex.	78206	727 E. Durango, Rm A-513	(512) 229-6250
	RO	Kansas City	Mo.	64106	911 Walnut St., 23rd Floor	(816) 374-3318
	DO	Kansas City	Mo.	64106	1150 Grande Ave. - 5th Floor	(816) 374-5557
	DO	Des Moines	Iowa	50309	New Federal Building, 210 Walnut St., Room 749	(515) 284-4422
VII	DO	Omaha	Neb.	68102	Nineteen and Farnam Streets, Empire State Building	(402) 221-4691
	DO	St. Louis	Mo.	63101	Suite 2500, Mercantile Tower, One Mercantile Center	(314) 425-4191
	DO	Wichita	Kan.	67202	110 East Waterman Street, Main Place Building	(316) 267-6566
VIII	RO	Denver	Colo.	80202	Executive Tower Bldg, 1405 Curtis Street	(303) 837-0111
	DO	Denver	Colo.	80202	721 19th St., Room 426A	(303) 837-0111

SBA FIELD OFFICES: ADDRESSES AND TELEPHONE NUMBERS (cont'd)

REGION		CITY	STATE	ZIP CODE	ADDRESS	(TELEPHONE NUMBERS FOR PUBLIC USE ONLY)
	DO	Casper	Wyo.	82601	Federal Building, Room 4001, 100 East B. St.	(307) 265-5550
	DO	Fargo	N. Dak.	58102	Federal Building, 653 2nd Ave., North, Room 218	(701) 783-5771
	DO	Helena	Mont.	59601	618 Helena Avenue	(406) 588-6011
VIII	DO	Salt Lake City	Utah	84111	Federal Building, 125 South State St., Room 2237	(801) 588-5500
	DO	Sioux Falls	S. Dak.	57102	National Bank Building, 8th & Main Ave., Room 402	(605) 336-2980
	BO	Rapid City	S. Dak.	57701	515 9th St., Federal Bldg. 246 (Rm.)	(605) 343-5074
	RO	San Francisco	Calif.	94102	Federal Building, 450 Golden Gate Ave., Box 36044	(415) 556-4530
	DO	San Francisco	Calif.	94105	211 Main Street	(415) 556-9000
	BO	Fresno	Calif.	93721	Federal Building, 1130 O. St., Room 4015	(209) 487-5000
	POD	Sacramento	Calif.	95825	2800 Cottage Way	(916) 484-4200
IX	DO	Las Vegas	Nev.	89121	301 E. Stewart	(702) 385-6011
	POD	Reno	Nev.	89504	300 Booth Street	(702) 784-5234
	DO	Honolulu	Hawaii	96813	1149 Bethel St., Room 402	(808) 546-8950
	BO	Agana	Guam	96910	Ada Plaza Center Building	**(-) 777-8420
	DO	Los Angeles	Calif.	90071	350 S. Figueroa St., 6th Floor	(213) 688-2000
	DO	Phoenix	Ariz.	85004	112 North Central Ave.	(602) 261-3900
	DO	San Diego	Calif.	92188	880 Front Street, Federal U.S. Building, Room 4-S-33	(714) 293-5444

201

SBA FIELD OFFICES: ADDRESSES AND TELEPHONE NUMBERS (cont'd)

REGION	CITY	STATE	ZIP CODE	ADDRESS	(TELEPHONE NUMBERS FOR PUBLIC USE ONLY)
RO	Seattle	Wash.	98104	710 2nd Ave., 5th Floor, Dexter Horton Building	(206) 442-1455
DO	Seattle	Wash.	98174	915 Second Ave., Federal Building - Room 1744	(206) 442-5534
DO	Anchorage	Alaska	99501	1016 West 6th Ave., Suite 200, Anchorage Legal Center	(907) 272-5561
X					
BO	Fairbanks	Alaska	99701	501½ Second Avenue	**(907) 452-1951
DO	Boise	Idaho	83701	216 North 8th St., Room 408	(208) 554-1096
DO	Portland	Oreg.	97205	1220 S.W. Third Avenue, Federal Building	(503) 221-2682
DO	Spokane	Wash.	99210	Court House Building, Room 651	(509) 456-2100

10 Regional Offices (RO)　　18 Branch Offices (BO)

63 District Offices (DO)　　15 Post-of-duty (POD)

**Dial Operator for Assistance

202

ECONOMIC DEVELOPMENT ADMINISTRATION: UNITED STATES DEPARTMENT OF COMMERCE

Sources of Information

Atlantic Regional Office

Room 10424, 600 Arch Street
Philadelphia, Pennsylvania 19106
(215) 597-4603

**Economic Development
Representatives' Offices**

Room 10424, 600 Arch Street
Philadelphia, Pennsylvania 19106
(215) 597-4603

60 Washington Street
Hartford, Connecticut 06106
　Brooklyn, New York, and
　Rhode Island are also served by this office.

213 Federal Building
40 Western Avenue
Augusta, Maine 04330
　Vermont is also served by this office.

Room 103, 1419 Forest Drive
P.O. Box 1667
Annapolis, Md. 21401
(301) 267-0890

441 Stuart Street
Boston, Massachusetts 02116

8002 Federal Office Building
400 North Eighth Street
Mailing: P.O. Box 10053
Richmond, Va. 23240

204 Federal Office Bldg.
55 Pleasant Street
Concord, New Hamp. 03301
(603) 225-6450

501 Federal Building
402 East State Street
Trenton, New Jersey 08608
　Delaware is also served by this office.

Room 939, 100 State Street
Albany, New York 12207

Room 407, Pan American Building,
255 Ponce de Leon Avenue
Hato Rey, San Juan, Puerto Rico 00917
　Virgin Islands are also served by this
　office.

304 New Post Office Building
West Pike Street
Clarksburg, West Virginia 26301
　Serves Northeastern West Virginia.

B-020 Federal Building
Beckley, West Virginia 25801
　Serves Southern West Virginia.

Suite 319, Prichard Building
601 Ninth Street
Huntington, West Virginia 25701
　Serves Western West Virginia.

Mailing: P.O. Box 1277
Huntington, W. Va. 25701

Midwestern Regional Office

32 West Randolph Street
Chicago, Illinois 60601
(312) 353-7706

**Economic Development
Representatives' Offices**

Suite D, 606 East Main Street
Carbondale, Illinois 62901
Mailing: P.O. Box 1136
Carbondale, Ill. 62901

Room 110, Century Building
36 South Pennsylvania Street
Indianapolis, Indiana 46204

306 Capital Savings and Loan Building
112 East Allegan Street
Lansing, Michigan 48933
　Serves Lower Michigan.

Room 407, Federal Building
515 West First Street
Duluth, Minnesota 55802
    Serves Eastern Minnesota.

415 Federal Building
Bemidji, Minnesota 56601
    Serves Western Minnesota.

405 Security Bank Building
Athens, Ohio 45701

Room 32, 510 South Barstow
Eau Claire, Wisconsin 54701
(715) 834-9508
    Upper Michigan is also served by
    this office.

Rocky Mountain Regional Office

Suite 505, Title Building
909 17th Street
Denver, Colorado 80202
(303) 837-4714

**Economic Development
Representatives' Offices**

Suite 505, 909 17th Street
Denver, Colorado 80202
    Wyoming and Kansas are also served
    by this office.

201 Crestwood Bank Building
9705 U.S. Highway 66
St. Louis, Missouri 63126
    Iowa is also served by this office.

339 Federal Office Building
North Main Street
Butte, Montana 59701

FARMERS HOME ADMINISTRATION: UNITED STATES DEPARTMENT OF AGRICULTURE

Sources of Information

Alabama
Rm. 717, Aronov Bldg., 474 South Court St.
Montgomery, AL 36104
(205) 832-7077

Arizona
Rm. 6095, Federal Bldg.,
230 North First Ave.
Phoenix, AZ 85025
(602) 261-3191

Arkansas
5529 Federal Office Bldg.
700 West Capital
Little Rock, AR 72201
(501) 378-6281

California
(Hawaii)
459 Cleveland St.,
Woodland, CA 95695
(916) 449-3223, 666-2650

Colorado
Rm. 231, No. 1 Diamond Plaza,
2490 West 26th Ave.
Denver, CO 80211
(303) 837-4347

Delaware
(District of Columbia, Maryland,
New Jersey)
Robscott Bldg.
151 East Chestnut Hill Rd.
Suite 2
Newark, DE 19711
(302) 731-8310

Florida
Room 214, Federal Bldg.
401 S.E. First Ave.
Gainesville, FL 32602
(904) 376-3210

Georgia
355 E. Hancock St.
Athens, GA 30601
(404) 546-2162

Idaho
Rm. 429, Federal Bldg., 304 N. Eighth St.
Boise, ID 83702
(208) 342-2711, Ext. 664

Illinois
2106 W. Springfield Ave.
Champaign, IL 61820
(217) 356-1891

Indiana
Suite 1700, 5610 Crawfordsville Rd.
Indianapolis, IN 46224
(317) 269-6415

Iowa
Rm. 873, Federal Bldg., 210 Walnut St.
Des Moines, IA 50309
(515) 284-4121

Kansas
536 Jefferson St.
Topeka, KS 66607
(913) 234-8661, Ext. 375

Kentucky
333 Waller Ave.
Lexington, KY 40504
(606) 252-2312, Ext. 2733

Louisiana
3727 Government St.
Alexandria, LA 71301
(318) 448-3421

Maine
USDA Office Bldg.
Orono, ME 04473
(207) 866-4929

Michigan
Rm. 209,
1405 South Harrison Rd.
East Lansing, MI 48823
(517) 372-1910, Ext. 272

Minnesota
U.S. Courthouse, 252 Federal Office Bldg.
St. Paul, MN 55101
(612) 725-5842

Mississippi
Rm. 830, Milner Bldg.
Jackson, MS 39201
(601) 969-4316

Missouri
Parkade Plaza, Terrace Level
Columbia, MO 65201
(314) 442-2271, Ext. 3241

Montana
Federal Bldg.,
P.O. Box 850,
Bozeman, MT 59715
(406) 587-5271, Ext. 4211

Nebraska
Room 308 Federal Bldg.
100 Centennial Mall North
Lincoln, NE 68508
(402) 471-5551

New Mexico
Rm. 3414, Federal Bldg.,
517 Gold Ave., S.W.
Albuquerque, NM 87102
(505) 766-2462

New York
Rm. 214, Midtown Plaza
700 East Water St.,
Syracuse, NY 13210
(315) 473-3458

North Carolina
Rm. 514, Federal Bldg.
310 New Bern Ave.
Raleigh, NC 27601
(919) 755-4640

North Dakota
P.O. Box 1737
Bismarck, ND 58501
(701) 225-4011, Ext. 4237

Ohio
Rm. 448, Old Post Office Bldg.
121 E. State St.,
Columbus, OH 43215
(614) 469-5606

Oklahoma
Agricultural Center Office Bldg.
Stillwater, OK 74074
(405) 372-7111, Ext. 239

Oregon (Alaska)
Rm. 1590, Federal Bldg.
1220 S.W. 3rd Ave.
Portland, OR 97204
(503) 221-2731

Pennsylvania
Rm. 728,
Federal Bldg., 228 Walnut St.,
P.O. Box 905
Harrisburg, PA 17108
(717) 782-4476

Puerto Rico
(Virgin Islands)
G.P.O. Box 6106G,
San Juan, PR 00936
(809) 722-3508

South Carolina
P.O. Box 21607
Columbia, SC 29221
(803) 765-5876

South Dakota
P.O. Box 821
Huron, SD 57350
(605) 352-8651, Ext. 355

Tennessee
538 U.S. Court House Bldg.,
801 Broadway
Nashville, TN 37203
(615) 749-7341

Texas
3910 South General Bruce Drive
Temple, TX 76501
(817) 773-1711

Utah (Nevada)
Rm. 5311, Federal Bldg.,
125 South State St.
Salt Lake City, UT 84138
(801) 524-5027

Vermont
(Connecticut, Massachusetts,
New Hampshire, Rhode Island)

141 Main St., P.O. Box 588
Montpelier, VT 05602
(802) 223-2371

Virginia
P.O. Box 10106
Richmond, Va 23240
804-782-2451

Washington
Rm. 319 Federal Office Bldg.
301 Yakima St.,
Wenatchee, WA 98801
(509) 663-0031, Ext. 353

West Virginia
P.O. Box 678
Morgantown, WV 26505
(304) 296-3791

Wisconsin
Suite 209, 1st Financial Place
1305 Main St.
Stevens Point, WI 54481
(715) 341-5900

Wyoming
P.O. Box 820
Casper, WY 82601
(307) 265-5550, Ext. 3272

FEDERAL RAILROAD ADMINISTRATION: UNITED STATES DEPARTMENT OF TRANSPORTATION

Sources of Information

Connecticut
Connecticut Dept. of Transportation
24 Wollcott Hill Road
P.O. Drawer A
Wethersfield, Connecticut 06109
(203) 566-4675

Delaware
Division of Transportation
P.O. Box 788
Dover, Delaware 19901
(302) 678-4593

District of Columbia
D.C. Dept. of Transportation
415-12th St., N.W.
Washington, D.C. 20004
(202) 629-4412

Illinois
Illinois Dept. of Transportation
2300 S. Dirksen Parkway
Springfield, Ill. 62764
(217) 782-5123

Indiana
Center for Urban and Regional Analysis
Indiana University
1022 East Third Street
Bloomington, Indiana 47401
(812) 337-7874

Maryland
Rail Systems Section
Maryland Dept. of Transportation
P.O. Box 8755
Baltimore, Maryland 21240
(301) 768-9520 Ext. 235

Massachusetts
Massachusetts Executive Office of
   Transportation and Construction
1 Ashburton Street
Boston, Massachusetts 02108

Michigan
Bureau of Transportation
P.O. Drawer K
Lansing, Michigan 48904
(517) 373-9580

New Hampshire
New Hampshire Office of
   Comprehensive Planning
State House Annex
Concord, New Hampshire 03301
(603) 271-3716

New Hampshire Public Utilities
   Commission
Railroad Division
26 Pleasant Street
Concord, New Hampshire 03301
(603) 271-3716

New Jersey
Division of Transportation
   Systems Planning
New Jersey Dept. of Transportation
1035 Parkway Avenue
Trenton, New Jersey 08625
(609) 292-6556

New York
Railroad Task Force
New York Dept. of Transportation
Building Five
State Campus
Albany, New York 12232
(518) 457-1176

Ohio
Bureau Statewide Systems Planning
Ohio Department of Transportation
Room 411
24 South Front Street
Columbus, Ohio 43215
(614) 466-2826 or 2122

Pennsylvania
Pennsylvania Dept. of Transportation
Room 1220
Commonwealth and Forster Streets
Harrisburg, Pa. 17120
(717) 787-3154

Vermont
Vermont Agency of Transportation
133 State Street
Montpelier, Vermont 05602
(802) 828-2828

Virginia
State Transportation Coordinator
Virginia Dept. of Highways and
    Transportation
1401 E. Broad Street
Richmond, Virginia 23219
(804) 786-2861

West Virginia
West Virginia Railroad
    Maintenance Authority
Room 223
922 Quarrier Street
Charleston, West Virginia 23505

WEIGHTS AND MEASURES

UNIT	ABBR. OR SYMBOL	EQUIVALENTS IN OTHER UNITS OF SAME SYSTEM	METRIC EQUIVALENT
		weight	
		avoirdupois	
ton			
short ton		20 short hundredweight, 2000 pounds	0.907 metric tons
long ton		20 long hundredweight, 2240 pounds	1.016 metric tons
hundredweight	cwt		
short hundredweight		100 pounds, 0.05 short tons	45.359 kilograms
long hundredweight		112 pounds, 0.05 long tons	50.802 kilograms
pound	lb *or* lb av *also* #	16 ounces, 7000 grains	0.453 kilograms
ounce	oz *or* oz av	16 drams, 437.5 grains	28.349 grams
dram	dr *or* dr av	27.343 grains, 0.0625 ounces	1.771 grams
grain	gr	0.036 drams, 0.002285 ounces	0.0648 grams
		troy	
pound	lb t	12 ounces, 240 pennyweight, 5760 grains	0.373 kilograms
ounce	oz t	20 pennyweight, 480 grains	31.103 grams
pennyweight	dwt *also* pwt	24 grains, 0.05 ounces	1.555 grams
grain	gr	0.042 pennyweight, 0.002083 ounces	0.0648 grams
		apothecaries'	
pound	lb ap	12 ounces, 5760 grains	0.373 kilograms
ounce	oz ap *or* ℥	8 drams, 480 grains	31.103 grams
dram	dr ap *or* ʒ	3 scruples, 60 grains	3.887 grams
scruple	s ap *or* ℈	20 grains, 0.333 drams	1.295 grams
grain	gr	0.05 scruples, 0.002083 ounces, 0.0166 drams	0.0648 grams

UNIT	ABBR. OR SYMBOL	EQUIVALENTS IN OTHER UNITS OF SAME SYSTEM	METRIC EQUIVALENT
		capacity	
		U.S. liquid measure	
gallon	gal	4 quarts (231 cubic inches)	3.785 liters
quart	qt	2 pints (57.75 cubic inches)	0.946 liters
pint	pt	4 gills (28.875 cubic inches)	0.473 liters
gill	gi	4 fluidounces (7.218 cubic inches)	118.291 milliliters
fluidounce	fl oz *or* f ℥	8 fluidrams (1.804 cubic inches)	29.573 milliliters
fluidram	fl dr *or* f ℨ	60 minims (0.225 cubic inches)	3.696 milliliters
minim	min *or* ♏	1/60 fluidram (0.003759 cubic inches)	0.061610 milliliters
		U.S. dry measure	
bushel	bu	4 pecks (2150.42 cubic inches)	35.238 liters
peck	pk	8 quarts (537.605 cubic inches)	8.809 liters
quart	qt	2 pints (67.200 cubic inches)	1.101 liters
pint	pt	1/2 quart (33.600 cubic inches)	0.550 liters
		British imperial liquid and dry measure	
bushel	bu	4 pecks (2219.36 cubic inches)	0.036 cubic meters
peck	pk	2 gallons (554.84 cubic inches)	0.009 cubic meters
gallon	gal	4 quarts (277.420 cubic inches)	4.545 liters
quart	qt	2 pints (69.355 cubic inches)	1.136 liters
pint	pt	4 gills (34.678 cubic inches)	568.26 cubic centimeters
gill	gi	5 fluidounces (8.669 cubic inches)	142.066 cubic centimeters
fluidounce	fl oz *or* f ℥	8 fluidrams (1.7339 cubic inches)	28.416 cubic centimeters
fluidram	fl dr *or* f ℨ	60 minims (0.216734 cubic inches)	3.5516 cubic centimeters
minim	min *or* ♏	1/60 fluidram (0.003612 cubic inches)	0.059194 cubic centimeters

UNIT	ABBR. OR SYMBOL	EQUIVALENTS IN OTHER UNITS OF SAME SYSTEM	METRIC EQUIVALENT
		length	
mile	mi	5280 feet, 320 rods, 1760 yards	1.609 kilometers
rod	rd	5.50 yards, 16.5 feet	5.029 meters
yard	yd	3 feet, 36 inches	0.914 meters
foot	ft *or* '	12 inches, 0.333 yards	30.480 centimeters
inch	in *or* "	0.083 feet, 0.027 yards	2.540 centimeters
		area	
square mile	sq mi *or* m^2	640 acres, 102,400 square rods	2.590 square kilometers
acre		4840 square yards, 43,560 square feet	0.405 hectares, 4047 square meter
square rod	sq rod *or* rd^2	30.25 square yards, 0.006 acres	25.293 square meters
square yard	sq yd *or* yd^2	1296 square inches, 9 square feet	0.836 square meters
square foot	sq ft *or* ft^2	144 square inches, 0.111 square yards	0.093 square meters
square inch	sq in *or* in^2	0.007 square feet, 0.00077 square yards	6.451 square centimeters
		volume	
cubic yard	cu yd *or* yd^3	27 cubic feet, 46.656 cubic inches	0.765 cubic meters
cubic foot	cu ft *or* ft^3	1728 cubic inches, 0.0370 cubic yards	0.028 cubic meters
cubic inch	cu in *or* in^3	0.00058 cubic feet, 0.000021 cubic yards	16.387 cubic centimeters

METRIC SYSTEM[1]

LENGTH

unit	abbreviation	number of meters	approximate U.S. equivalent
myriameter	mym	10,000	6.2 miles
kilometer	km	1,000	0.62 mile
hectometer	hm	100	109.36 yards*
dekameter	dam	10	32.81 feet
meter	m	1	39.37 inches
decimeter	dm	0.1	3.94 inches
centimeter	cm	0.01	0.39 inch
millimeter	mm	0.001	0.04 inch

AREA

unit	abbreviation	number of square meters	approximate U.S. equivalent
square kilometer	sq km or km^2	1,000,000	0.3861 square mile
hectare	ha	10,000	2.47 acres
are	a	100	119.60 square yards
centare	ca	1	10.76 square feet
square centimeter	sq cm or cm^2	0.0001	0.155 square inch

VOLUME

unit	abbreviation	number of square meters	approximate U.S. equivalent
dekastere	das	10	13.10 cubic yards
stere	s	1	1.31 cubic yards
decistere	ds	0.10	3.53 cubic feet
cubic centimeter	cu cm or cm^3 also cc	0.000001	0.061 cubic inch

METRIC SYSTEM[1]

CAPACITY

unit	abbreviation	number of liters	approximate U.S. equivalent		
			cubic	*dry*	*liquid*
kiloliter	kl	1,000	1.31 cubic yards		
hectoliter	hl	100	3.53 cubic feet	2.84 bushels	2.64 gallons
dekaliter	dal	10	0.35 cubic foot	1.14 pecks	1.057 quarts
liter	l	1	61.02 cubic inches	0.908 quart	0.21 pint
deciliter	dl	0.10	6.1 cubic inches	0.18 pint	0.338 fluidounce
centiliter	cl	0.01	0.6 cubic inch		0.27 fluidram
milliliter	ml	0.001	0.06 cubic inch		

MASS AND WEIGHT

unit	abbreviation	number of grams	approximate U.S. equivalent	
metric ton	MT *or* t	1,000,000	1.1 tons	
quintal	q	100,000	220.46 pounds	
kilogram	kg	1,000	2.2046 pounds	
hectogram	hg	100	3.527 ounces	
dekagram	dag	10	0.353 ounce	
gram	g *or* gm	1	0.035 ounce	
decigram	dg	0.10	1.543 grains	
centigram	cg	0.01	0.154 grain	

Prefix	Symbol	Multiple*	deci-	d	10^{-1}
			centi-	c	10^{-2}
deka-	da	10	milli-	m	10^{-3}
hecto-	h	10^2	micro-	μ	10^{-6}
kilo-	k	10^3	nano-	n	10^{-9}
mega-	M	10^6	pico-	p	10^{-12}
giga-	G	10^9	femto-	f	10^{-15}
tera-	T	10^{12}	atto-	a	10^{-18}

*10^{-1} means 0 1 Similarly 10^{-6} = 0 000001 etc. 10^3 = 1 000
10^6 = 1 000 000 etc.

Table I. Measurement Units

Length

U.S. Customary Unit	U.S. Equivalents	Metric Equivalents
inch	0.083 foot	2 54 centimeters
foot	1/3 yard. 12 inches	0 3048 meter
yard	3 feet. 36 inches	0 9144 meter
rod	5 1/2 yards. 16 1/2 feet	5 0292 meters
mile (statute, land)	1.760 yards. 5.280 feet	1 609 kilometers
mile (nautical, international)	1.151 statute miles	1 852 kilometers

Area

U.S. Customary Unit	U.S. Equivalents	Metric Equivalents
square inch	0.007 square foot	6 4516 square centimeters
square foot	144 square inches	929 030 square centimeters
square yard	1.296 square inches. 9 square feet	0 836 square meter
acre	43.560 square feet. 4.840 square yards	4 047 square meters
square mile	640 acres	2 590 square kilometers

Volume or Capacity

U.S. Customary Unit	U.S. Equivalents	Metric Equivalents
cubic inch	0.00058 cubic foot	16 387 cubic centimeters
cubic foot	1.728 cubic inches	0 028 cubic meter
cubic yard	27 cubic feet	0 765 cubic meter

U.S. Customary Liquid Measure	U.S. Equivalents	Metric Equivalents
fluid ounce	8 fluid drams. 1.804 cubic inches	29 573 milliliters
pint	16 fluid ounces. 28.875 cubic inches	0 473 liter
quart	2 pints. 57.75 cubic inches	0 946 liter
gallon	4 quarts. 231 cubic inches	3 785 liters
barrel	varies from 31 to 42 gallons, established by law or usage	

U.S. Customary Dry Measure	U.S. Equivalents	Metric Equivalents
pint	1/2 quart. 33.6 cubic inches	0 551 liter
quart	2 pints. 67.2 cubic inches	1 101 liters
peck	8 quarts. 537.605 cubic inches	8 810 liters
bushel	4 pecks. 2.150 42 cubic inches	35 238 liters

British Imperial Liquid and Dry Measure	U.S. Customary Equivalents	Metric Equivalents
fluid ounce	0.961 U.S. fluid ounce. 1.734 cubic inches	28 412 milliliters
pint	1.032 U.S. dry pints. 1.201 U.S. liquid pints. 34.678 cubic inches	568 26 milliliters
quart	1.032 U.S. dry quarts. 1.201 U.S. liquid quarts. 69.354 cubic inches	1 136 liters
gallon	1.201 U.S. gallons. 277.420 cubic inches	4 546 liters
peck	554.84 cubic inches	0 009 cubic meter
bushel	1.032 U.S. bushels. 2.219.36 cubic inches	0 036 cubic meter

Weight

U.S. Customary Unit (Avoirdupois)	U.S. Equivalents	Metric Equivalents
grain	0.036 dram. 0.002285 ounce	64 79891 milligrams
dram	27.344 grains. 0.0625 ounce	1 772 grams
ounce	16 drams. 437.5 grains	28 350 grams
pound	16 ounces. 7,000 grains	453 59237 grams
ton (short)	2,000 pounds	0 907 metric ton (1 000 kilograms)
ton (long)	1.12 short tons. 2.240 pounds	1 016 metric tons

Apothecary Weight Unit	U.S. Customary Equivalents	Metric Equivalents
scruple	20 grains	1 296 grams
dram	60 grains	3 888 grams
ounce	480 grains. 1.097 avoirdupois ounces	31 103 grams
pound	5.760 grains. 0.823 avoirdupois pound	373 242 grams

SELF ASSESSMENT

Throughout the book we have talked about many different things, some technical, some not technical. The following questions should be used as a test for you to give yourself. These questions should be answered thoughtfully and truthfully.

1. After reading the manual are you willing to get the necessary training by taking courses which will require time away from your family and will limit your leisure time? Would you consider taking a job working in the industry?

2. Have you fully considered the money aspect of this endeavor? How much will you need? How much can you borrow?

3. Do you feel that customers will patronize the type restaurant you are considering opening? Is the concept right for the area in which restaurant will be located?

4. Do you feel that you will be able to get the project off the ground?

5. Can you picture yourself as the owner/operator managing and making all the decisions? Are you physically fit? How does your family feel about it?

6. How about the location? Have you one in mind? Does it measure up to what has been learned so far?

7. Where will you get your equipment needs and supplies? If you are starting off with equipment already in service, what is the condition of the equipment?

8. Do you understand fully the purpose of good bookkeeping? Have you decided whether you will be taking care of this or having someone else do it?

9. Do you have a plan to take care of all your legal and insurance matters?

10. What plans do you have to acquire necessary techniques or knowledge of purchasing, pricing, budgeting, advertising, training and management?

In a previous chapter we talked about a man who was an excellent chef but failed as a restaurant owner primarily because he didn't take the time to learn all the other facets of the business. Don't fall into the same trap. *Learn, be advised, act.*

QUESTIONS

1.   What must be done before doing any business?

2.   Who must purchase Workmens' Compensation insurance?

3.   What does Workmens' Compensation insurance cover?

4.   Before selling at retail you must register with 1) ___ and 2) ___ .

5.   What items must be withheld from employees' wages?

6.   What kinds of insurance are needed to protect the business?

7.   Name some agencies that could be contacted for additional information.

18
Summary With No End

This book has no end since it is subject to change and is meant to be an ever-changing manual. This is not a cut and dried business. Food service is a dynamic, growing and changing business. This manual is meant to reflect just that to help you attain success.

The food service industry is a great business. I feel it is one of the most gratifying businesses one can get into. It is a people business (all kinds). It truly is a business that with effort, some learning and lots of determination you can be successful in and enjoy for many years, or find an excellent job in.

FUTURE OF BUSINESS AND SOME CHARACTERISTICS

At an early age one learns that eating out is a pleasant experience. It starts with the school lunch program and goes right on through adulthood. You will see many changes in the future. Hospitals are experimenting with opening their dining rooms to the public. Fast food chains are taking on contracts for feeding schools, factories, etc. Nutrition of items on menus will be given more attention. The eating public is more conservative today. The schools and colleges are turning out conservative students once again. This will affect the food service industry. More truth in advertising will be evident. We have learned that, despite a recession, the food service business still does well. Eating out has become a way of life as well as an experience and/or an adventure. Recently I read that the food service industry is going to be a 100 billion dollar industry very shortly.

The high cost of energy is a concern to everyone in the food service business. This can be a big problem to a restaurant operator in the future as well as in the present depending on how high it goes.

The future will also bring about mandatory training for owners and employees in areas of sanitation, licensing and other areas to protect the public. The day may come when a chef or cook may be required to have a license similar to plumbers, hairdressers, etc. before they can get a job.

A SUMMARY OF WHAT MAKES THE RESTAURANT SUCCESSFUL

Success in the restaurant business both now and in the future is based on the following:

1. The area in which the restaurant is located.

2. How well the owner operates his/her business be it a steak house, hamburger stand, etc. You have to realize that basically what the public is looking for is good food, excellent service, a clean restaurant value and a good trained staff. These are the things that will bring them back again and again. The fixtures, the painting of the walls, tasteful decorative effects all help but the basics are what keep it together and make a profit for the owner.

TRENDS

The volume of the restaurant business is expected to increase substantially over the next decade. This is because people have more leisure time and because higher wages are being earned by today's generation versus past generations. The family is also eating out more because so many women are now working. With the cost of buying and preparing food at home, in many instances, it is cheaper to eat out. Opportunities for employment in the industry will be high.

The food service industry will have its problems attracting good help just as it has in the past. A restaurant owner must know how to obtain good people and train them.

Success in this business is not guaranteed. In comparison to some other businesses restaurant failures are high. Remember that you are more capable than you think you are and in a restaurant you can become successful by demonstrating your ability, by learning all you can and by working hard.

FRANCHISING TREND

Franchising will grow. You will see possible extensions of present menu offerings. If a franchise route is the one you want to take there will be many opportunities available.

IN CONCLUSION

Over 55,000 new restaurants have opened in the United States since 1974. Self-service and car service restaurants accounted for the largest increase.

Table and counter service restaurants accounted for the second largest increase. Everything from pizza parlors, Chinese, Japanese, German and other ethnic type restaurants plus the standard type restaurants are all on the increase. The future is ripe. The timing is good. You are on the right track by reading this manual. The rest is up to you.

Although you see many big chains in the restaurant business it is still dominated by the small operator giving truth to the saying that there are more small fish in the ocean than big ones.

Today, more than ever before, people are getting better advice and suggestions on how to run a restaurant. They are going into more debt to pay for it but they are willing to listen, learn and act which is part of being successful in any business. The ratio of restaurant failures is going down.

Running a restaurant has its personnel problems and shortage of trained kitchen people. No other type of business you could get into is more demanding and small things as mentioned in this manual that go unchecked can put you out of business.

I strongly suggest that you now reread this manual with a paper and pencil handy and write down all questions you have on things that are not clear to you and get the answers.

I think this is a romantic business even with all its problems. Very few businesses offer a chance to meet so many different types of people who are enjoying good food, pleasant surroundings and are making a profit for you.

At times this business requires that you must do many things but approach them with an open mind. If the dishroom attendant doesn't come in, you're elected. The same goes for cook, baker, cashier, etc.

You must always be receptive to learning new things, investigating new products, equipment, etc. This keeps you abreast of the times and the industry.

QUESTIONS

1. Success in the restaurant business is based on _____ and _____ .

2. Why is the restaurant business expected to increase over the next decade?

3. It is easy to attract good help in food service industry.

   True ___   False ___

4. Over 55,000 new restaurants have opened in U.S. since 1974.

   True ___   False ___

5. Table and counter service accounted for the largest increase.

6. If dishroom attendant doesn't come in the cook will usually fill in.

   True ___   False ___

PERSONAL MESSAGE

Vocational education or career education will become more universal as the years pass.

The food service industry will be offering this training early in the student's learning career.

Countries like the Soviet Union are now stressing vocational education more than ever.

Going into business for yourself or going into a career is a big step so if I can help you in any way feel free to write to me and I will answer your questions as soon as possible.

Good Luck, Happiness and Health.

19
Analysis and Evaluation Report

The author has used this report in his consultant work.

The teacher can use it as an excellent class project in determining the plus or minus of an existing food service location or a new food service location.

This also lets the student know what type of service a professional food service consultant can offer.

This type of report properly administered can help evaluate the degree of success a business will have.

This can also be administered for the buyer, the seller or a lending institution.

This type of information presented to insurance companies, attorneys, lending institutions or government agencies will label the one making the presentation as a professional.

Presenting this type of report will usually result in success.

A Food Service Industry

"ANALYSIS AND EVALUATION REPORT"

FOR _____(Name and address_____

_____of business)_____

_____

_____

Prepared by _____

Ray Petteruto

_____Food Service Consultant_____

Date _____January 20 – 1961 S.A.P._____

TABLE OF CONTENTS

I FOOD SERVICE LOCATION

1. *Competition*
   (a) Short potential of proposed Food Service in re: competition and location.
       Reason:

   (b) Long potential of proposed Food Service in re: competition and location.
       Reason:

   (c) In immediate area—similar type of competition—their success.

   (d) Size of Food Service competition—estimated volume, which location is seemingly superior? Why?

   (e) Future competition based on need for this business in area—or Country.

2. *Parking Lot*
   (a) Food Service competition's parking lots re: size—location—accessibility—expansion features in comparison to proposed new Food Service location.

   (b) Parking lot space in terms of present inside seating capacity and expansion plans. Ramp availability for wheelchair customers.

3. *Food Service Approach*
   (a)   Visibility away and from all angles of business.

   (b)   Visibility vs. competition—plus and minus of both.

   (c)   Traffic pattern of Food Service business being a growth, one or other.
         Reason:

4. *Value of Location*
   (a)   With Food Service—completely equipped.

   (b)   Without Food Service—equipment.

   (c)   Other possible use of this location instead of Food Service—if need be.

   (d)   This new use would be based on what?

   (e)   Does concept offered add to area and is it needed?

5. *Food Service Utilities*
   (a)   Water, gas, electricity, sewerage, snow removal services, etc. Maintenance methods to be used. In case of breakdowns, type of person on calling-in basis—their reputation in the field.

6. *High Points of Food Service Location*
   Reasons:

7. *Low Points of Food Service Location*
   Reasons:

SUMMARY AND SUGGESTIONS RE: "LOCATION"

II FOOD SERVICE PROJECTIONS

RE: Sales, labor, food costs, expenses and proposed net profit.

All above are broken down in percentages to sales and are evaluated as to their probability and obtainability.

We require these projection figures submitted to us to accomplish above plus complete indebtedness and ability to add more to business, if need be, by future restaurant owner.

SUMMARY AND SUGGESTIONS RE: "PROJECTIONS"

III PROPOSED FOOD SERVICE TREND

1. Trend of this Food Service business in this area.

2. Trend of this Food Service business nationally.

3. How long has this Food Service trend been offered—locally and nationally?

4. What dangers exist to this Food Service trend—locally and nationally? Why?

5. What is the concept to be presented?

SUMMARY AND SUGGESTIONS RE: "FOOD SERVICE TREND"

IV MENU—ANALYSIS

1. *Pricing*
   (a) How selling price is determined.

   (b) Competitive—to others using same type menu.

   (c) Does area warrant this type of food pricing?

2. *Type of Food*
   (a) Owner's ability to make up all items, if need be.

   (b) Acceptance of food—to be established—or existing?

   (c) What is owner using to insure standardization of food in purchasing, preparation and service of food?

OWNER TRAITS (FOOD SERVICE)

1. *Background*
   (a) Food service knowledge.

   These findings based on investigation with people who know owner.

   (b) Attitude.

   To determine if owner is actively engaged in business. Owner's attitude an asset or a liability?

(c)   Appearance.

Conducive to the Food Service business pressures and pace.

(d)   Other fact-finding items.

(e)   Ability to merchandise, supervise, schedule, book-keeping.

(f)   Owner's apparent desire to succeed. What writer feels it is based on.

(g)   Emergency.

In case of a long-term sickness what would happen to management?

(h)   In case of death?

SUMMARY AND SUGGESTIONS RE: "OWNER TRAITS"

VI FOOD SERVICE LAYOUT AND EQUIPMENT

1. Entire layout of business re: Wasted steps, future expansion, capacity, quality, workability and cost. Number of seats.

2. Type of Food Service employees using equipment and their training in efforts to prevent accidents and equipment breakdown.

3. Type of layout vs. competition in immediate area.

4. In case of power failure is there an auxiliary unit available?

5. If an entire power failure did occur, what serious effect would this have to the cash flow of the business?

VII FOOD SERVICE SECURITY

1. *Supervision*
   (a) In absence of owner.
   (b) Is replacement experienced?
   (c) Were they trained? By whom?

2. *Stockroom*
   (a) Method of reorder?
   (b) Is stockroom locked and in separate area?
   (c) Who, other than owner, has accessibility to stockroom?
   (d) Is food stored to insure quality — health protection?
   (e) Is there sufficient ventilation to deter spoilage in stockroom?
   (f) Quality brands of all foods and supplies used.

3. *Employees*
   (a) Personnel check when employee handles cash. Type of check used.

   (b) Methods used in handling cash—all levels.

   (c) Control of time with clock or book. Kept by whom?

   (d) Does this meet state requirements for Labor Wage laws?

   (e) Do they have a copy of the state law posted?

   (f) Who hires and trains new employees?

4. *Premises*
   (a) Any alarms for robbery or fire? Are they adequate? Name and type.

   (b) Deep Fryer duct system having fire extinguisher nearby or not?

   (c) Does everyone know its use?

5. *Suppliers*
   (a) Their reputation—quality—required payment.

(b)   Established vendors. List names, addresses.

(c)   Who checks in items?

(d)   What times are deliveries set for?

(e)   Who pays bills?

(f)   Method of paying bills—cash or check?

SUMMARY AND SUGGESTIONS RE: "SECURITY"

VIII RECORD KEEPING

1. *Type*
   (a) Evaluate — good and bad points.
   (b) Will there be an accountant available?
   (c) Is accountant experienced from prior exact knowledge of this type business?
   (d) Are items tracked week to week re: their usage vs. salescheck cross-check?

   By whom? Accountant's letter of affiliation attached herein.

SUMMARY AND SUGGESTIONS RE: "RECORD KEEPING"

IX LEGAL—INSURANCE

1. *Protective Structure re:*
   (a) Accidents.

   (b) Liabilities, etc.

2. *Product liability needed*

3. *State and local licenses*

4. *Health cards, laws abided by*

5. Does owner have an attorney? Name and address? List some other Food Service operations attorney has advised. Attorney's letter of affiliation attached herein.

6. Did attorney find out all necessary laws involved with this business?

7. Did they consult an insurance company re: all avenues of protection for this business? List name, address, date spoken to. Date coverage started.

SUMMARY AND SUGGESTIONS RE: "LEGAL—INSURANCE"

X FOOD SERVICE PREPARATION

1. Method used to establish consistency of quality in preparation.

2. Preparation area in re: expansion.

3. Equipment in relationship to actual work in preparation area.

4. In the event of major breakdown, what other methods are quickly available for refrigeration, electricity, Deep Fryers, urns, ovens, etc.?

SUMMARY AND SUGGESTIONS RE: "PREPARATION"

XI PICTURES

1. *Photos*

    (a) Inside and out

    (b) Of nearby competition

    (c) Of surrounding area

PICTURE COMMENT

XII FOOD SERVICE BUILDING

1. Sketch included

2. Type of construction

3. Approximate size

4. Yearly upkeep costs. What can lower them?

5. Evaluated in terms relative to similar type businesses in same value area.

6. *Air Conditioning*
   - (a) Adequate?
   - (b) Air conditioning in terms of future expansion.
   - (c) Type being used in proposed location. Name and make.

7. *Heat*
   - (a) Type.
   - (b) Heat in terms of future expansion.
   - (c) Name and make.
   - (d) Location of heating plant in building.
   - (e) Approximate yearly cost of operation.
   - (f) Does this meet all laws re: heating regulations?

8. *Directions posted*
   Listing all water shut-offs, all emergency telephone numbers and emergency preventative items used.

9. Drainage and angle re in: washroom floors, parking lot and real estate.

10. *Electrical System*
    - (a) Name of installer.
    - (b) Electrical system re: future expansion.

11. *Rest Rooms*
    - (a) Relationship to all areas in proximity of food service building.
    - (b) Adequate?

12. Any law enforcement measures needed evenings, weekends, at grand opening? Cost of service.

SUMMARY AND SUGGESTIONS RE:
"FOOD SERVICE BUILDING"

Bibliography of Government Publications on Food Service Industry and Related Subjects

☐ Alcohol is a Drug, There are 9,000,000 Alcohol Addicts in America. *Colored Poster.* 1972. 16 x 14 in. HE 20.2421:A1 1 017-024-00189-9 $ .75

• • • • • • • • •

☐ Armed Forces Recipe Service, Including Changes 1 – 3. 1969, reprinted 1976. 1038 cards, each 5 x 8 in. D 101.11:10–412/2/rep. 008-020-00608-4
21.00

☐ Change 4 to above. 1976. 271 cards, each 5 x 8 in. D 101.11:10-412/2/ch.4 008-020-00593-2   5.00

☐ Index to Recipes. 1976. 93 p. D 101.11:10-412/2/ind./ 976 008-020-00594-1
3.70

• • • • • • • • •

☐ Baking for People With Food Allergies. *A booklet of special recipes that eliminate wheat, eggs, or milk from the diets of people who are allergic to one or more of these foods. The recipes have all been tested for quality.* Rev. 1975. 12 p. il. A 1.77:147/2 001-000-03362-0   .35

☐ Calories and Weight, the USDA Pocket Guide. *This handy pocket guide lists calorie values of meal size portions of meats, breads, vegetables, beverages, and snacks. Very useful for persons with a limited daily caloric intake.* 1974. 100 p. il. A 1.75:364 001-000-03172-4   1.00

☐ The Chemistry of Food Safety. 1973. 8 p. il. HE 20.4010/A:F 739/2 017-012-00195-5   .35

□ Clean Hands. *Stresses the importance of clean hands by demonstrating, through illustrations, the proper method of washing hands.* 1972. 14 p. il. HE 20.4002:C 58 017-012-00145-9   .35

□ Composition of Foods, Raw, Processed, Prepared. *This publication includes information useful in estimating the nutrient values of food and presents 5 tables of data on composition of foods — edible portions of 100 grams, edible portions of 1 pound as purchased, selected fatty acids, cholesterol and magnesium content. Data is given for energy, proximate composition, Vitamin A, thiamine, riboflavin, niacin, ascorbic acid, calcium, phosphorus iron sodium, and potassium.* Reprinted 1975. 190 p. A 1.76:8/963 001-000-00768-8 $ 3.60

□ Cooking for Small Groups. *This meal planning guide offers tips on adjusting recipes to group sizes, keeping food safe to eat, and preparing salads and desserts.* 1974. 22 p. il. A 1.75:370 001-000-03210-1   .35

•••••••••

Daily Food Guide, Some Choices for Thrifty Families: *Colored Posters.*

□ Large Poster. Reprinted 1970. 28 x 22 in. A 98.9:13/poster 001-024-00121-0
.35

□ Small Poster. Reprinted 1973. 8 x 10 1/2 in. A 98.9:13/2 001-024-00199-6
.35

□ Spanish edition to above. 1970. 8 x 10 1/2 in. A 98.9:13-S/2 001-024-00203-8
.35

•••••••••

□ Dare to Excel in Cooking, Award Winning Group Recipes of USS Semmes (DDG-118), Winner of the 1966 Ney Award. *These recipes designed to yield 25 portions include soups; salads and dressings; poultry; meats, sauces and fish; cheese and eggs; vegetables; beverages; pies, cakes and pastry. Conversion tables for smaller portions are provided.* Reprinted 1975. 52 p. il. D 201.2:C 77 008-040-00001-0   .85

□ Development Document for Effluent Limitations Guidelines and New Source Performance Standards for the Animal Feed, Breakfast Cereal, and Wheat Starch, Segment of the Grain Mills Point Source Category. 1975. 115 p. il. EP 1.8/3:An 5 055-001-01007-9   1.90

□ Did You Really Wash Your Hands? Wash Thoroughly, Sanitize Properly, Dry Carefully Before Handling Food or Utensils, Clean Food Production Requires Clean Hands. *Colored Poster.* 1971.   20 x 15 in.   HE 20.4021:H 19 017-012-00132-7   .75

☐ Diet Manual. *A series of diets approved for use at Hines Veterans Administration Hospital and Foster C. McGaw Hospital, Loyola University of Chicago. Assists hospital staff as a reference providing nutritional care.* 1976. 165 p., looseleaf. VA 1.10:d 56 051-000-00093-5 $ 2.45

☐ Dishwashing. *Describes the various types of dishwashing machines; the preparation of dishes for dishwashing; special treatment of various types of dinnerware; machine maintenance and repair; and the various types of quality dishwashing compounds and rinse additives.* 1971. 25 p. il. GS 2.2:D 63/971 022-001-00031-1   .65

☐ Evaluation of Dishwashing Systems in Food Service Establishments. 1973. 34 p. il. A 1.82:1003 001-000-02971-1   .50

☐ Fats in Food and Diet. Rev. 1976. 10 p. il. A 1.75:361/3 001-000-03568-1
                                                                                                     .35

☐ Federal Food, Drug, and Cosmetic Act as Amended, January 1976. *Contains the text of the Federal Food, Drug, and Cosmetic Act as amended to incorporate all amendments through May 1976.* 1976. 149 p. HE 20.4005:F 73/976 017-012-00239-1   1.70

☐ Food Allergy. 1975. 12 p. il. HE 20.3252:F 73 017-044-00012-5
                                                                                                     .35

☐ Food and Nutrition. (Bimonthly.) *Reports on the Federal food assistance programs administered by the Food and Nutrition Service. It shows their impact on people, the activities of public and private agencies in helping those in need of food assistance, and outstanding work of individuals or groups of volunteers in furthering the drive to eliminate malnutrition in the U.S.* Subscription price: Domestic – $3.00 a year, 50¢ single copy; Foreign– $3.75 a year, 65¢ single copy. (FN-File Code 2N) A 98.11:

☐ Food and Nutrition, A Problem Centered Approach. 1976. 20 p. A 1.68:1008 001-000-02485-0   .55

☐ Food and Nutrition, The 1959 Yearbook of Agriculture. Clothbound. 736 p. il. A 1.10:959 001-000-00106-0   7.85

☐ Food and Your Weight. *Here's a book crammed with tips on sensible eating. It includes a table of calorie values in most common foods, a chart of proper body weights for men and women, suggestions on computing your daily calorie requirements, and plans for people desiring to lose or gain weight.* Rev. 1973. 38 p. il. A 1.77:74/5 001-000-03601-7   .50

☐ Food Buying Guide for Child Care Centers. Rev. 1977. 43 p. il. A 98.9:108/2
001-024-00206-2 $ 1.00

☐ Food Chart, Child Care Food Program. 1977. A 1.68:1165 001-000-03669-6
.50

☐ Food for Fitness, A Daily Food Guide. Rev. 1973. 8 p. il. A 1.35:424/6
001-000-02882-1   .35

☐ Food for the Teenager During Pregnancy. *A colorful, easy-to-read guide for
young pregnant women, providing advice on weight gain, nutrition, planning
meals, food groups, vitamins, and more.* 1976. 24 p. il. HE 20.5102:P 91/2
017-026-00036-4   .80

☐ Food For Us All, The 1969 Yearbook of Agriculture. *How to buy and cook
food, with full details. Meals planning and ways to achieve better nutrition
for you and your family. The economics of food. These are the main topics
of a book that celebrates the glories of food with practical know-how that
every homemaker can put to good use.* Clothbound. 1969. 400 p. il.
A 1.10:969 001-000-00116-7   5.95

☐ Food Selection for Good Nutrition in Group Feeding. *This publication is
primarily for the use of food consultants, nutritionists, and others who help
food managers and administrators in resident institutions to plan for meals
that are nutritionally adequate and satisfying and that are within the money
allowance.* Rev. 1972. 32 p. A 1.87:35/2 001-000-02633-0   .65

☐ Has Anyone You Care About Changed for No Apparent Reason? *May be used
as a poster.* 1970, reprinted 1973. 20 p. il. J 24.2:Is 1   027-004-00002-4
.35

☐ Hashish, Pot, Acid, and Speed, Barbiturates, LSD, Will They Turn You On or
Will They Turn On You. *Colored Poster.* 1970, reprinted 1972. 28 x 22 in.
HE 20.2421:W 66 017-024-00087-6   .80

☐ Health and Safety Guide for Retail Bakeries. 1975.   52 p. il., 2 pl.
HE 20.7108/2:B 17 017-033-00049-2   1.10

☐ Home Delivered Meals. *For the elderly, a program of home delivered meals
can often make the difference between being able to remain in their homes
and going into an institution. The rapid growth of such programs prompted
the Administration on Aging to sponsor this selected annotated bibliography.*
1974. 25 p. HE 1.212:M 46 017-046-00025-0   .80

☐ How to Use USDA Grades in Buying Food. Rev. 1977. 15 p. il. A 1.77:196/2
001-000-03652-1   .35

☐ The Human Heart: A Living Pump. *A colorful folder of non-technical information about the operation and function of the heart and circulatory system.* 1976. 6 p., folder. HE 20.3202:H 35/9 017-043-00067-6 $ .35

☐ If It's Cold, Keep It Cold! *Poster.* 1974. 20 x 30 in. (Fold to 10 x 7 1/2 in.) HE 20.4021:C 67 017-012-00204-8   .35

☐ If It's Hot, Keep It Hot! *Poster.* 1974. 20 x 30 in. (Fold to 10 x 7 1/2 in.) HE 20.4021:H 79 017-012-00205-6   .35

●●●●●●●●●●

☐ Include These Foods in the Lunch Each Day, Serve Each Child a Real Type "A". *Poster.* Rev. 1969. 8 x 11 in. A 98.9:4 *OUT OF PRINT*

☐ Spanish edition of above. Rev. 1970. 8 x 11 in. A 98.9:4-S 001-024-00116-3 .35

Institutional Meat Purchase Specifications. *The U.S. Department of Agriculture, through its Meat Grading Service, makes available to institutional users of meat an Acceptance Service designed to assure such persons that meats they purchase comply with detailed specifications approved by USDA. One publication in this series prescribes general requirements for the inspection, packing, packaging, acceptance and delivery of meat products and the others contain descriptions of the various meat products customarily purchased by institutional users of meat.*

☐ General Requirements. 1971, reprinted 1976. 7 p. A 88.17/4:R 29/971 001-016-00076-8   .35

☐ For Cured, Dried and Smoked Beef Products, Series 600. Rev. 1976. 6 p. A 88.17/4:B 39/2/976 001-016-00102-1   .35

☐ For Cured, Smoked and Fully Cooked Pork, Series 500. 1971, reprinted 1976. 7 p. A 88.17/4:P 82/3/971 001-016-00073-3   .35

☐ For Edible By-Products, Series 700. 1973. 4 p. A 88.17/4:B 99/971 001-016-00020-2   .35

☐ For Fresh Beef, Series 100. Reprinted 1974. 15 p. il. A 88.17/4:B 39/975 001-016-00095-4   .45

☐ For Fresh Lamb and Mutton, Series 200. Reprinted 1974. 3 p. il. A 88.17/4:L 16/975 001-016-00096-2   .35

☐ For Fresh Pork, Series 400. Reprinted 1974. 5 p. il. A 88.18/4:P 82/975 001-016-00097-1   .35

☐ For Fresh Veal and Calf, Series 300. 1975. 8 p. il. A 88.18/4:V 48/975
001-016-00098-9 $ .35

☐ For Sausage Products, Series 800. Rev. 1976. 22 p. il. A 88.17/4:Sa 8/976
001-016-00101-1   .45

●●●●●●●●●●

☐ It's Good Food — Keep It Safe. 1973. 6 p. il. A 1.68:1057 001-000-02953-3
.35

☐ "John Was OK . . . Until His Momma Caught Him, Now He Can't Go Home
Anymore." *Colored Poster.* 1970. 18 x 16 in.   HE 20.2421:J 61
017-024-00083-3   .80

☐ Keeping Food Safe to Eat, A Guide for Homemakers. 1975.   10 p.
A 1.77:162/3 001-000-03396-4   .35

☐ Keeping Foods Clean. 1974. 4 p. il. HE 20.4010/A:F 739/3 017-012-00217-0
.35

☐ Know the Eggs You Buy. *A colored poster illustrating the different weight
classes of eggs and compares the quality of grades as they are broken out of
the shell, fried and poached.* Rev. 1968. 45 x 30 in. A 88.40/2:62
001-016-00067-9   .60

☐ Nursing Homes and Homes for the Aged, A Guide to Nutrition and Food Service. 1975. 110 p. il. HE 20.2558:N 95/971 017-001-00392-1   3.20

☐ Nutrients and Foods for Health: Flyer. *A chart that shows you some nutrients you need, what they do for you, and some foods that supply them.*
1973. 4 p. A 98.9:97 001-024-00183-0   .35

☐ Nutritive Value of American Foods in Common Units. 1975. 291 p. il.
A 1.76:456 001-000-03184-8   5.15

☐ Nutritive Value of Foods. 1975. 41 p. A 1.77:72/5 001-000-03493-6
1.00

☐ A Planning Guide for Food Service in Child Care Centers. *Designed to help
child care center directors and other personnel in the Child Care Food Program plan their food service. Gives a sample 10-day menu for children 3-6
years old.* Rev. 1976. 26 p. il. A 98.9:64/2 001-024-00205-4   .75

☐ Preliminary Findings of the First Health and Nutrition Examination Survey,
United States, 1971-72, Anthropametric and Clinical Findings. 1975. 82 p.
il. HE 20.6202:H 34/2/971-72 017-021-00026-5   1.45

☐ Prevention of Food Poisoning. *This book is designed for food service specialists and supervisors. It reveals the dangers of chemical and biological food poisoning, and discusses the causes and prevention of dysentery and trichinosis.* 1975. 102 p. il. D 106.22:0348 008-025-00025-8 $ 2.20

☐ Protect Food — Stay Alert. *This booklet has helpful suggestions for persons involved in food handling.* Reprinted 1974. 8 p. il. HE 20.4002:F 73/4 017-012-00151-3   .35

☐ Protecting Home-Cured Meat From Insects. Rev. 1974. 6 p. il. A 1.77:109/4 001-000-03212-7   .35

☐ Protecting Our Food, The 1966 Yearbook of Agriculture. *A story of how the quality and wholesomeness of our food is protected against insects, disease, decay and loss of body-building values. Includes facts for selecting and preparing food, the whys and hows of meat and poultry inspection, food grading, milk safeguards, the world and national food outlook and food problems in military and space operations.* Clothbound. 1966. 386 p. il. A 1.10:966 001-000-00113-2   5.85

☐ Quantity Recipes for Child Care Centers. *Designed to provide quantity recipes and other information for preparing meals in child care centers. The measurements for recipes are given for 50 servings.* 1973. 168 p. il. A 98.9:86 001-024-00170-8   6.40

☐ Quantity Recipes for Type A School Lunches, With Index Cards. Rev. 1971. 203 cards, each 5 x 8 in. A 1.68:631/3 001-000-00499-9   14.05

☐ Safe Handling of Foods in the Home. 1973. 12 p. il. HE 20.10/A: F 739 017-012-00193-9   .40

☐ Sanitation Guidelines for the Control of Salmonella in the Production of Fish Meal. 1971. 7 p. il. C 55.13:NMFS CIRC-354 003-020-00023-1   .40

☐ Slavery to Drugs (Black Version). *Colored Poster.* 1970, reprinted 1974. 11 x 21 in. HE 20.2421:S1 1 017-024-00085-0   .75

☐ Slavery to Drugs (White Version). *Colored Poster.* 1970, reprinted 1973. 11 x 21 in. HE 20.2421:S1 1/2 017-024-00086-8   .75

☐ So You Work in a Food Plant! *Emphasizes the importance of cleanliness and food sanitation practices on the part of food plant workers.* 1976. 12 p. il. HE 20.4002:F 73 017-012-00146-7   .40

☐ Starting and Managing a Small Drive-In Restaurant. Reprinted 1975. 65 p. il. SBA 1.15:23 045-000-00113-0   .90

☐ A Study of the Effect of Remuneration Upon Response in the Health and Nutrition Examination Survey, United States. 1975. 23 p. il. HE 20.6209:2/67
017-022-00402-0 $ .80

☐ Travelers' Tips on Bringing Food, Plants and Animal Products into the United States. Rev. 1976. 13 p. il. A 1.68:1083/3 001-000-03555-0   .35

☐ USDA Grade Standards for Food, How They are Developed and Used. *Includes a brief description of grading and inspection criteria, standards, and their development, and techniques for the various classifications of food sold commercially.* 1973. 22 p. A 1.68:1027/2 001-000-03326-3   .35

☐ USDA Grades Help You Choose. 1970. Portfolio of 10 colored posters, each 20 x 15 in. A 88.38:G 75 001-016-00071-7   3.75

☐ Watch out for Lead Paint Poisoning. Reprinted 1975. 3 p. HE 20.5102:P 75/2
017-030-00034-5   .35

●●●●●●●●●●

We Want You to Know About:

☐ Labels on Foods. 1973. 6 p. il. HE 20.4002:F 73/6 017-012-00183-1
.35

☐ Protecting Your Family From Foodborne Illness. 1973. 2 p. HE 20.4002:F 43/7 017-012-00189-1   .35

●●●●●●●●●●

☐ What Kind of a Drinker Are You? Take This Test and Find Out for Yourself. *Colored Poster.* 1972. 16 x 14 in. HE 20.2421:D 83 017-024-00188-1
.35

Glossary

Accounts receivable. The balance of money that is owed by debtors—but not necessarily cash in hand.

A la carte. All menu items that are priced separately, i.e. not a part of a pre-set menu.

A la king. Food that is served with or in a white sauce.

A la maison. Style of the house (restaurant).

Amandine (almond). Any dish made with almonds.

Arbitration. A dispute between parties is brought before one or more arbitrators, both parties agreeing beforehand to abide by the arbitrators decision.

Articles of incorporation. A legal document filed with the state setting forth the purpose and regulations of a corporation.

Assets. All resources, rights or items owned by an individual or corporation.

Au gratin. Any dish made with cheese.

Back of house. The area of a restaurant where food is prepared and where other activities take place relating to serving the customers' needs.

Back bar. Equipment opposite the serving counter.

Bain Marie, or sandwich unit. An arrangement of pans set in a table or counter top. The unit holds a water unit to keep foods hot.

Baked Alaska. A dessert made with cake and ice cream, topped with beaten, sweetened egg whites (meringue) and browned in an oven before serving.

Bill of fare. Menu listing items that are available for serving.

Boil in bag. A pouch that contains foods which are heated through by putting the pouch in boiling water for a specified time.

Break-even point. The point at which sales equal expenses.

Broiler, upright. A vertical broiler with an opening in the front.

Buffalo chopper. An automatic food chopper.

Buffet unit. A mobile or stationary counter or free-standing unit with heated wells or sections for hot dishes, as well as places for cold dishes, where food can be attractively displayed for self-service.

Café Royale. Coffee served with liqueur or brandy.

Candled eggs. Eggs that have been turned before a light to determine their quality.

Carbonator. Motor-driven water pump with control valve and tank. It mixes cold water and CO_2 gas in a storage tank to produce soda water.

Cash discount. A deduction given for prompt payment of a bill.

Casserole. A baked menu entrée dish usually consisting of meat, fish, poultry, vegetable(s).

Caviar. The roe(or eggs) of sturgeon or other fish, salted and served as an appetizer.

Château Briand. A thick filet mignon.

China, institutional or restaurant. China made with greater durability than regular household china.

Coffee grinder. A machine (generally motor-driven) with a bean hopper at the top that grinds coffee beans.

Coeur. Heart (French).

Club Sandwich. A combination sandwich made with three slices of bread, with different meats, cheeses etc. as the fillings.

Combination sandwich. Usually made with two items, for example ham and cheese, tuna with melted cheese etc.

Condiment. Any seasoning used to make food more flavorful.

Consommé. A clear soup.

Co-signer. A person who signs for a loan with the borrower, and in so doing guarantees that they will meet the obligation if the borrower defaults.

Creole Sauce. A savory sauce cooked with tomatoes, green peppers, onions and seasonings.

Crêpe. A thin egg pancake.

Crêpes Suzette. Thick egg pancake flamed with liqueur or brandy.

Croutons. Small cubes of dried bread used as a garnish with cream soups or on salads.

Delmonico potatoes. Cubed potatoes baked in a cream sauce, topped with buttered crumbs.

Demitasse. A small cup in which after-dinner coffee is often served.

Depreciation. A loss in value of a building, equipment, car etc. as a result of deterioration, use, age, etc.

Detergent dispenser. Usually placed on top of dishwasher to dispense liquid soap.

Dough divider. Floor model, motorized, divides dough into equal sized pieces, which are then taken by conveyer to the next production stage.

Dressing, French. Generally consists of four measures of oil mixed with one measure of vinegar, seasoned with salt, paprika, pepper. Sometimes other spices are used, or onion juice may be added.

Dressing, Russian. One part chili sauce to two parts mayonaisse.

Dressing, Thousand Island. Chopped sweet pickle, vegetable oil, eggs, tomatoes, onion, celery, pimentoes, vinegar, sugar, salt, water and spices.

Du jour. "Of the day" (French).

Dunnage rack. Solid or louvered platform used for cases or bag items.

Escalloped. Food baked in a casserole with a sauce, often topped with bread crumbs.

En casserole. Food baked and served in the same dish.

Entrée. The main course.

Entrepreneur. An individual who owns and manages a business.

Espagnole. A basic brown sauce.

Expeditor. The person who checks all foods for proper make-up and distribution to those serving.

Expresso coffee. Italian style of coffee, made under steam pressure and served in a small (demitasse) cup.

Floater. An employee who fills in when a regular employee is out sick or on vacation.

Fondue. A dish made with grated, melted cheese, eggs, butter etc.

Franchise. Authorization given by an established company, to one or more persons, to sell the company's products or services.

Fricassee. Large pieces of chicken or meat served in a gravy or cream sauce.

Fromage. Cheese (French).

Front of house. The area of a restaurant where the customers are served.

Garnish. An edible item added to a dish for eye appeal, such as parsley, radishes, lemon slices, etc.

Gong brush. A short-handled pot brush.

Gross figures. The total amount of money received before expenses or debts are paid. There is a *great* difference between gross profit and net profit.

Hand service. A food service business where plates and glassware were carried by hand.

Hollandaise sauce. A creamy sauce made with egg yolks, melted butter and lemon juice and seasonings, served with vegetables or seafood.

Hors d'Oeuvres. An appetizer, generally served before a meal.

Hot water booster. Insulated tank or coil, to raise incoming hot water temperature to sanitary temperature—for sterilization purposes. The booster can be steam, electric or gas heated.

Jardinière. French word meaning "with vegetables."

Julienne. Meat or vegetables cut into thin strips.

Lease. A rental agreement between owner and a person or persons wishing to lease a certain property. It is usually for a number of years, depending upon what the parties have agreed upon.

Lyonnaise. Food that has been sliced or chopped and fried in butter with finely sliced or chopped onions.

Maraschino. Any food flavored or decorated with cherries preserved in syrup.

Marketing. The buying or selling of products or services.

Marmite. A beef consomme.

Mayonnaise. A thick, uncooked emulsion of edible vegetable oil, egg yolk, whole egg and vinegar or lemon juice or both, plus salt or other seasonings.

Meats and Poultry.

Baby beef. The trade term for the tender beef of young steers and heifers.
Beef. The meat of cattle approximately one year old or older.
Lamb. A general term referring to the flesh of sheep, either male or female, under one year of age.
Pork. Meat of hogs usually less than one year of age. The best pork comes from hogs 6 to 8 months of age.
Poultry. Chicken, turkey, duck, goose, fowl, guinea hen, squab, etc.
Veal. Meat of calves not over 12 weeks of age.

Menu mix. Group offering of types of food and price structure.

Microwave oven. An oven in which foods are cooked or heated through by absorbing microwave energy which is generated by magnetrons.

Mixed grill. Any combination of three kinds of meat on one plate.

Mocha. A combination of coffee and chocolate.

Monkey dish. A small dish usually used to serve vegetables, approximately 3 ½" in diameter.

Motivation. Influencing an employee to perform his/her work at the highest level of his/her ability.

Parfait server. A tall server used for a dessert similar in makeup to a sundae.

Parmesan cheese. A very hard cheese made in Italy from partly skimmed milk. It is cured for two years. It is often sold grated and will keep for years.

Pass-through window. An opening in the wall between the kitchen and serving area through which dishes can be passed.

Pickled. Any food that has been treated with salt, spices, vinegar, etc.

Pimentos. Sweet red peppers that have been steeped in a brine.

Plate covers. These are used to cover plates and dishes for sanitary purposes, and to keep food at the desirable temperature, either hot or cold.

Platform scale. Dial or beam type, used to weigh objects up to 1500 pounds.

Poached. To cook slowly in water or other liquid.

Pot rack. Used to store pots and pans when not in use.

Pot roast. To cook meat in water or other liquid, using a covered pan.

Poulet. Chicken (French).

Profit. Excess of returns over expenditures.

Puree. Any food that has been put through a sieve or strainer.

Ramekin. A shallow dish, usually with a handle, used for both baking and serving.

Roast. To cook meat in the oven (dry heat).

Roux. A thickening agent made from flour and fat.

Sauté. To pan fry quickly with butter, oil or other fat.

Sear. To put meat in an extremely hot pan or oven just long enough to brown and sear in natural juices.

Shirred. To bake plain or in milk in a buttered dish, as eggs.

Shoestring potatoes. Long strips of french fried white potatoes (Julienne style).

Simmer. To cook in water, just below the boiling point.

Smorgasbord. Scandinavian food buffet with many tasty items, including a variety of meats, fish and cheeses.

Souffle. A fluffy, light, baked dish made with eggs, milk and other ingredients. This must be served immediately or it will "fall" (lose its fluffy appearance and light texture).

Spumoni. Italian ice cream.

Staple products. All nonperishable grocery products.

Station. Table or counter area assigned to an employee.

Steam. To cook over boiling water, as in a double boiler.

Stew. To simmer slowly in a covered pan with water or other liquid.

Strudel. A style of European pastry.

Toss. (As a salad). To lift upwards with quick motions, using a fork and spinning the bowl at the same time. Or two forks can be used.

Tray service. All items served on trays, with care being given to distribution of weight.

Urn cup. Usually used to measure water when making coffee.

Vitrified china. The process that gives American china its strength.

NOTE: Different terminology may be used in different parts of the country.

Operational Data

Food as Purchased

Tomatoes	20 lbs. per flat
	6 lb. till = 12/24 tomatoes
Lettuce	24 heads per box
String Beans	28 lbs. per bushel
Spinach	20 lbs. per bushel
Carrots	48 lbs. per bag
Celery	24-30-36 or 48 heads to a crate
Grapefruit	18-23-27-32 or 40 per crate
Pineapple	9-12-15-18 or 24 per crate
Oranges	California, 56-72-80 or 100 per box
	Florida, 88-100 or 125 per box
Strawberries	12 pints per flat
Bananas	6 lbs. per hand, as a rule
Eggs	30 dozen to a case
Eggs, small	weigh 17 oz. or more per dozen
Eggs, medium	weigh 20 1/2 oz. or more per dozen
Eggs, Large	weigh 24 oz. or more per dozen
Eggs, extra large	weigh 26 oz. or more per dozen
Eggs, Jumbo	weigh 28 oz. or more per dozen

Equivalency Chart

Item	Ounces per cup
Butter	7 3/4
Grated Cheese	4
Egg Whites (8)	8
Egg Yolks	8
Flour (Unsifted)	4 3/4
Flour (Sifted)	4 1/4
(This is bread flour)	
Milk, liquid	8 1/2
Nuts, ground	4 1/4
Nuts, shelled	4
Raisins,	5 1/4
Rice	7
Shortening	7
Water	8
Sugar, granulated	7
Sugar, powdered	5

# of tin	Average net weight	# cups in contents
#10	6 lbs. 10 oz.	12 to 13 cups
# 5	3 lbs. 8 oz.	5 3/4 cups
#2 1/2	28 oz.	3 1/2 cups
# 2	20 oz.	2 1/2 cups
# 1 tall	16 oz.	2 cups

Soup-Sauce Ladles

Size	Equivalent to
1 ounce	1/8 cup
2 ounces	1/4 cup
4 ounces	1/2 cup
6 ounces	3/4 cup
8 ounces	1 cup

Oven Temperatures

Very hot	$475/500^{\circ}$
Hot	$425/450^{\circ}$
Moderately Hot	400°
Moderate	$350/375^{\circ}$
Moderately Slow	325°
Slow	$250/300^{\circ}$

Abbreviations Generally used

Teaspoon	tsp.
Tablespoon	Tbs.
Cup	C.
Pint	Pt.
Quart	Qt.
Peck	Pk.
Bushel	Bu.
Ounce/Ounces	Oz.
Pound/Pounds	Lbs.
Square	Sq.
Minute/Minutes	Min.
Dozen	Doz.

Food Service Pans—All Purpose

Size	Approximate measurements
Full size	12 3/4" by 20 3/4"
Half size	10 3/8" by 12 3/4"
Two thirds size	13 3/4" by 11 3/4"
One third size	6 7/8" by 10 3/8"
One sixth size	6 7/8" by 6 1/4"

Food Service Industry
Magazines and Newspapers

Airline Food & Flight Service, Airline News, Inc. 665 Lavilla, Miami Springs, Fl 33166, 305/887-1701. 6x/yr., *Personnel:* Alex Morton, Publ.; Lou Billingslea, Adv. Dir.; Alex Morton, Mktg.; Margie Tingley, Assoc. Ed. *Special Issues:* Who's Who in Airline Food (May); Who's Who—Supplier, Vendor (Nov.); Annual Report on Airlines (Jan.).

Canadian Hotel & Restaurant, McLean-Hunter Publ., 481 University Ave., Toronto M5W 1A7, Ont., Canada, 416/595-1811.

Chef Institutional, Culinary Review, 441 Lexington Ave., New York, NY 10017, 212/986-3390. 8x/yr.; chefs only (USA & Overseas). *Personnel:* George Serra, Publ.; Barbara Johnson, Ed. & Assoc. Publ. *Special Issues:* Concept in Food (May/June); Buyers Guide (Jan./Feb.). *Sales & Marketing Aids;* 6 issues published as directories. College/University (Dec.); Hospital (March); 100 Presidents (Jan./Feb.); NY Metro Buyer's Dir. (May); Convention & Banquet Fac. (July); Air Chef (Sept). Also: full-time test kitchen plus product seal of approval panel.

Catering Industry Employee, 120 E. 4th St., Cincinnati, OH 45202, 513/621-0300. *Personnel:* John P. Lavin, Ed. Magazine of The Hotel-Restaurant Employees & Bartenders Union (AFL-CIO).

Club & Food Service Magazine, Executive Business Media, Inc., PO Box 788, Lynbrook, NY 11563, 516/887-1800. 12x/yr. *Personnel:* John J. Ryan, publ.; Wm. C. Keeley, Natl. Adv. Mgr.; Peter A. Spina, Reg. Adv. Mgr.; Glenn E. Flood, Ed.; Melanie Kubat, food ed. *Special Issues:* Military Food Service Update (Jan.); Food Service Equipment Mfg. Directory (May & Nov.); Wine Issue (Aug.); Amer. Logistics Assn. Convention (Oct.) *Market Studies:* The Military Food Service Market.

Club Executive, R & W Mgmt. Co., 1028 Connecticut Ave. NW, Washington, DC 20036, 202/296-4514. 12x/yr. *Personnel;* Paul E. Reece, Pub. & Ed.; Wm. Vallee, Sls. Mgr.; Karen Herrington, Assoc, Ed. *Special Issues:* Buyer's Guide (Feb.); Almanac & Directory (Sept.).

Club Manager, Commerce Publ. Co., 408 Olive St., St. Louis, MO. 63102, 314/421-5445. 12x/yr. *Personnel:* Johnson Poor, publ., Eldon Miller, Ed.; Deborah Walther food editorial. *Special Issues:* CMAA Conference Issue (April); NRA Show (May); Equip. & Interiors (Oct.); Hotel Show (Nov.). *Sales & Marketing Aids:* Equipment Purchases by Clubs; Food Purchases by Private Clubs; Liquor Sales by Clubs. All free.

Commercial Kitchen & Dining Room, US Industrial Publications, Inc., 209 Dunn Ave., Stamford, CT 06905, 203/322-7676.

Cooking For Profit, Gas Magazines, Inc., 1202 S. Park St., Madison, Wis. 53715, 608/257-4656. 12 issues/yr.; *Key Personnel:* Edward J. Mayland, publ.; Richard W Johnson, Natl. Sls. Mgr.; David A. Mayland, Mktg. Dir.; James R. Myers, Ed. Dir.; Helen Sanstadt, Food Editorial. *Special Issues:* Jan., 4/c product gallery; Mar., sanitation; Apr. Dessert-O-Rama; May, NRA convention; July, school lunch focus; Sept., frying; Oct., table top & hotel show. *Special Services:* Annual Profit Guide of Foodservice Equipment, various editorial reprints; industry book department; product usage studies on fee basis through editorial department.

Cornell Hotel & Restaurant Administration Quarterly, School of Hotel Administration, Cornell University, Ithaca NY 14850, 607/265-5093. 4 issues/yr. Circ., 5,000. US & overseas. *Key Personnel:* Dean Robert A. Beck, Exec. Ed.; Prof. Helen J. Recknagel, Mng. Ed. *Special Services:* Bibliography for Hotels & Restaurants & Related Subjects (Aug.); Seminar & meeting list every issue; reprint service (list available).

Drive-in Fast Service, Harcourt Brace Jovanovich, Inc., 757 Third Ave., New York NY 10017, 212/754-3300, 12x/yr., *Personnel:* Lawrence Witchel, Pub.; Thomas Farr, Ed.

Food & Equipment Product News, Young/Conway Publ., Inc., 347 Madison Ave., New York NY 10017, 212/689-6850. 9x/yr. *Personnel:* Webb Young, Ed. & Pub.; Art Conway, Assoc. Pub.; Rich Conway, Natl. Accounts Mgr.; Peggy Legband, Assoc. Ed. (food). *Special Issues:* Western Buyers Directory & Annual Product Review (Jan./Feb.); Western Market Analysis (Apr.); Western NRA Show (June/July); Western Distribution Analysis (Aug.); NAFEM Show (Sept.); Hotel Show (Oct.) *Sales & Marketing Aids:* Sales Action/Inquiry Studies; Reader Idea Exchange Studies; contract market research.

Food Executive, Food Service Executives Assn., 508 IBM Bldg., Fort Wayne, Ind. 46805, 219/484-1901. 6x/yr. Circ.: 9,000. *Personnel:* Carleton B. Evans, Ed. & Pub.; Lucille L. Zink, Staff Exec.; Tina Brasher, Assoc. Ed. (food).

Food Management, Harcourt Brace Jovanovich, 757 Third Ave., New York NY 10017, 212/754-3100. 12x/yr. *Personnel:* Robert Edgell, Pub.; Lawrence Witchel, Assoc. Pub.; Ron Kramer, Natl. Sls. Mgr.; Art Bailey, Eastern Sls. Mgr.; William Patterson, Editor; Tom Farr, Sr. Ed. (food). *Special Issues:* Annual Equipment Previews/NAFEM (Sept.); Outlook (Jan.); Schools (coincides with ASFSA convention); Hospitals (coincides with ADA convention).

Sales & Marketing Aids: Institutional Market Trends.

Foodservice & Hospitality, Suite 807, 94 Cumberland St., Toronto, Ont. M5R 1A3, Canada, 416/923-8888. 12x/yr. *Personnel:* Mitch Kostuch, Pub. *Sales & Marketing Aids:* Canada's Hospitality Business; The Food Service Top '50'; Leaders in Hotel/Motel Lodging; Franchising in Foodservice & Lodging; Portfolio of Hospitality Advertising; Why advertise to the Hospitality Market; Media File.

Foodservice Distributor Salesman, Canners Publ. Co., 5 S. Wabash Ave., Chicago IL 60603, 312/372-6880, 12x/yr. bound into Institutions/VF. *Personnel:* Paul Considine, Pub.; John Corcoran, Ed.

Foodservice Equipment Dealer, Canners Publ. Co., 5 S. Wabash Ave., Chicago, IL 60603, 312/372-6880, 12x/yr. *Personnel:* Paul Considine, Pub.; Russ Carpenter, Ed. Dir. *Special Issues:* NRA Show (April); NAFEM Show (Aug.); Buyer's Guide (Oct.) Layout & Design (June/Sept./Dec.)

Food Service Marketing, EIP, Inc., Box 1648, Madison, Wis. 53701, 608/ 244-3528. 12x/yr. *Personnel:* Phillip L. Rane, Pub.; Tom Huth, VP, Mktg.; Michael Duval, Dir. Res.; Evelyn Evans, Ed. *Special Issues:* Annual Forecast (Jan.); Dir. of Systems Capability (May); Best of the Year (Dec.). *Sales & Marketing Aids:* Gallup Customer Surveys (1966-present); operator survey of check averages (dinner, luncheon, breakfast); survey of liquor usage among commercial establishments. Other services include advertisement readership studies, inquiry follow-up studies; special market research.

Frozen Food Age, (Food Service Market Section), 230 Park Ave., New York NY 10017, 212/639-9294, 12x/yr. *Personnel:* A. H. Rosenfeld, Pub.; Duane Shelton, Ed.

Health Care Product News, 125 Elm St., PO Box 696, New Canaan, Conn. 06840, 203/966-5691. 12x/yr. *Personnel:* Robt. J. Dowling, Pub.; Theodus Carroll, Ed.

Hospitals, Journal of The American Hospital Assn., 840 N. Lake Shore Dr., Chicago, IL 60611, 312/645-9400. 24x/yr. *Personnel:* D. S. Schecter, Ed.; Richard M. Dudley, Dir. Sls.

Hotel & Motel Management, Robert Freeman Publ. Corp., 845 Chicago Ave., Evanston, IL 60202, 312/328-4111. 12x/yr. *Personnel:* Robt. C. Freeman, Publ.; Robt. F. Schroeder, Midwest Sls. Mgr.; Joanne Pastirik, Mg. Ed. *Special Issues:* Beverage Merchandising (Dec.); Buyers Directory (Feb.).

Institutional Distribution, Restaurant Business, Inc., 633 Third Ave., New York NY 10017, 212/986-4800. 12x/yr. *Personnel:* Donald A. Karas, Pub.; Stanley J. Romaine, Assoc. Pub.; Robert Civin, Ed. & Assoc. Pub.; Janice Garr, Food Ed. *Special Issues:* Annual Survey of the Industry (Jan.); Annual Innovative Distributor Awards (Mar.); Industry Leaders Survey (May); Great Distributor Organization Study (June); The Top 50 Foodservice Distributors

(Dec.). *Sales & Marketing Aids:* Marketing & Purchasing Guide 1975/6; Profile of a Distributor Salesman; other services: contract market research; test kitchen.

Institutions/Volume Feeding, Cahners Publ. Co., 5 S. Wabash Ave., Chicago, IL 60603, 312/372-6880. 24x/yr. *Personnel:* David S. Wexler, Publ.; Paul Considine, Assoc. Pub.; Ed Fanter, Sales Dir.; Don Haynes, Mktg. Dir.; Jane Wallace, Ed. *Special Issues:* Executive Status (Winter); Convenience Foods (Sept.); Equipment Census (March); Menu Census (April); Institutions/VF 400 (July 15); Growth Chains (Jan.); NRA Show, Ivy Awards (May 1); Chargemaker (Oct.); Liquid Assets Alcoholic beverage demographics (6 times/yr.). *Sales & Marketing Aids:* Annual Menu Census; Annual Equipment Census; Annual Convenience Foods Study; Annual Single Service Study. Also: special proprietary market studies, market presentations, special tabs on the annual studies.

Journal of American Dietetic Assn., 420 N. Michigan Ave., Chicago, IL 60611, 312/822-0330, 12x/yr. *Personnel:* Dorothea F. Turner, Ed.; Bernell Halnel, Adv. Dir.

Kitchen Planning, Harcourt Brace Jovanovich, 757 Third Ave., New York NY 10017, 212/754-3300, 4x/yr., *Personnel:* Lawrence Witchel, Pub.

Military Market: Commissary Edition, Army Times Publ. Co., 475 School St., SW, Washington DC 20024, 202/554-7180, 12x/yr. *Personnel:* John H. O'Leary, Pub., Gerald F. McConnell, Ed.; Nancy M. Tucker, Assoc. Ed. (food). *Special Issues:* Buyers Guide to Suppliers (Jan.); Directory of Trade Names (July). *Sales & Marketing Aids:* Almanac (2.50).

Modern Healthcare, McGraw-Hill Publ., 230 W. Monroe St., Chicago IL 60606, 312/368-6621. 12x/yr. *Personnel:* Daniel M. Kelley, Pub.; Ted Isaacson, Ed.; Walter Nohstadt, Mktg. Sv.

Modern Schools, EIP Inc., PO Box 1648, Madison Wis. 53701, 608/244-3528. 9x/yr., *Personnel:* Phillip L. Rane, Pub.; Jeanne Connors, Ed.

Nation's Restaurant News, Lebhar-Friedman, Inc., 2 Park Ave., New York, NY 10016, 212/689-4800. 25x/yr. *Personnel:* David Q. Mahler, Group Publ. Dir.; Thomas Haas, Assoc. Publ.; Michael Schweitzer, Ed.; Charles Bernstein, Ex. Ed.; *Special Issues:* NRA Show (April); Distribution (July & Aug.); MUFSO (Sept., Oct.); Contract Food Service (Oct.); Hotel/Motel Show (Nov.); Frozen Food (Dec.).

Nation's Schools & Colleges, McGraw-Hill Publ., 230 W. Monroe St., Chicago, IL 60606, 312/368-6500, 10x/yr. *Personnel:* Daniel M. Kelley, Pub.; Loren Hickman, Ed.; Walter Nohstadt, Mktg. Dir.

Quick Frozen Foods (Instl. Foodservice Section), 757 Third Ave., New York NY 10017, 212/754-4337. 12x/yr. *Personnel:* Saul Beck, Co-Publ. & Natl. Adv. Mgr.; Sam Martin, Co-Publ. & Ed.

Resort Management, PO Box 4169, Memphis, Tenn. 38104, 901/276-5424. 12x/yr. *Personnel:* Allen J. Fagans, Ed.; Ramsey Pollard, Adv. Mgr.

Restaurant Hospitality Magazine, Patterson Publ., 614 Superior Ave. W., Cleveland, OH 44113, 216/696-0300. 12x/yr. *Personnel:* Wallace Patterson, Publ.; Shelden Jones, Sls. Mgr.; Bob de San, Mktg. Mgr; Stephen Michaelides, Ed.; Ronna Averbach, Assoc. Ed. (food). *Special Issues:* Product Reference File (Jan.); Alcoholic Beverages (March); Cost of Operations (Oct.); Top of Table (Nov.). *Sales & Marketing Aids:* Marketing Planbook.

Restaurant Business, Restaurant Business, Inc., 633 Third Ave., New York NY 10017, 212/986-4800. 12x/yr. *Personnel:* Donald A. Karas, Publ; Jeffrey P. Berlind, Assoc. Publ.; Joan Bakos, Ed. & Assoc. Publ.; Janice Garr, Food Editor. *Special Issues:* Franchising Annual (March);NRA Show (May);Restaurant Growth Issue (Sept.); Sanitation (Dec.). *Sales & Marketing Aids:* Market Research Studies on 1) glass & disposable ware; 2) frozen entrees; 3) coffee; 4) permanent ware; 5) butter/margarine; 6) beer. Restaurant Growth Index. Also: test kitchen (product evaluation & testing); food photography; sales promotion, creative & merchandising services; RB Advisory Panel studies available monthly.

School Product News, Industrial Publishing Co., 614 Superior Ave. W., Cleveland, OH 44113, 216/696-0300.

School Foodservice Journal, Amer. School Food Service Assn., 4101 E. Iliff Ave, Denver, Colo. 80222, 303/757-8555. Circ. 54,888. *Key Personnel:* Dr. John N. Perryman, Publ. & Exec. Dir.; Gordon Speckman, Mktg. & Sls. Dir. *Special Issues:* pre-convention issue (June); post-convention issue (Oct.); Back-to-School issue (Sept.). *Sales & Marketing Aids:* fact sheet available free; Marketing Newsletter.

Today's Chef/Food Service Executive, Cap News Inc., 149 Woodland Dr., Pittsburgh, PA 15236, 412/655-4993 or 412/892-2232. 8x/yr. *Personnel:* B. J. Mical, Ed. & Publ.; Sam Mical, Ex. V.P.; N. J. Colletti Sr., Co-Ed. (food). *Special Issues:* New Product (Jan./Feb.); NRA Show (Apr./May); President's Issue (July); Opportunity '75 (Nov./Dec.).

Truck Stop Management, Bobit Publ. Co., 1155 Waukegan Rd., Glenview Il 60025, 312/724-8440. 6x/yr. *Personnel:* E. J. Bobit, Publ; J. R. Dunlap, Asst. Publ.; Jim Dunlap, Ed.

Vending Times, Vending Times, Inc., 211 E. 43rd St., New York, NY 10017, 212/OX7-3868. 12x/yr. *Personnel:* Morris Weintraub, Publ.; Arthur E. Yohalem, Ed.; Tim Sanford, Food Ed. *Marketing & Sales Aids:* Buyer's Guide (Feb.); Census of The Industry (June).

OTHER MAGAZINE PROJECTS OF INTEREST

Food Processing Magazine, 430 N. Michigan Ave., Chicago IL 60611, 312/644-2020, Ray Hlavachek, Ed. Dir., Sept., 1975 to feature annual "Food Service Processing/Packaging" issue.

Progressive Grocer, 708 Third Ave., New York NY 10029, 212/490-1000, Robert E. O'Neill, Ex. Editor; William M. Ringler, Ed., Special Projects.

REGIONAL MAGAZINES, NEWSPAPERS

American Host, Box 3627, Des Moines Ia., 515/279-1725, 12x/yr. *Personnel:* Walter T. Proctor, Ed. & Publ.

The Chuck Wagon, Texas Restaurant Assn., P.O. Box 1429, Austin, Tex. 78767, 512/444-6543, 10x/yr. *Personnel:* Fred Williams, Ed.

Cirascope, Chicago & Ill. Restaurant Assn., 110 N. Wacker Dr., Rm. 208, Chgo IL 60606, 312/372-6200, 12x/yr. *Personnel:* Geo. L. Davidson, Publ; Susan Shinneman, Ed.

Food-Scope, c/o Archie Eagles, 1996 Eldridge W., Roseville, Minn. 55113, 612/631-2344. *Personnel:* Archie Eagles, Publ.

Lodging & Foodservice News, 131 Clarendon St., Boston, MA 02116, 617/267-9080. 26x/yr., *Personnel:* Harold Dolby, Ed./Publ.; Richard E. Dolby, Publ. Dir.

Metropolitan Restaurant News, 1225 Broadway, New York NY 10001, 212/689-5424. 12x/yr. *Personnel:* George Wattoff, Publ.; Morris Gut, Mg. Ed.

Pacific Northwest Restaurant News & Hotel Magazine, 6038 41st St., NE, Seattle WA 98115, 206, 525-9946. John F. Gordon, Publ.

Restaurant South, Box 9377, Greensboro, NC 27408, 919/288-4692, 12x/yr. *Personnel:* Emmet D. Atkins, Ed.; Herman G. Harris, Adv. Mgr.

Western Foodservice, Young/Conway Publications, 347 Madison Ave., New York NY 10017, 212/689-6850. 9x/yr. *Personnel:* R. P. Conway, Natl. Acct. Mgr.; Ted Miscnuk, Ed. (1709 W. 8th St., L.A., Cal. 213/483-3344).

Index

Index